MEDIEVAL TORTURE A

MODERN SEh

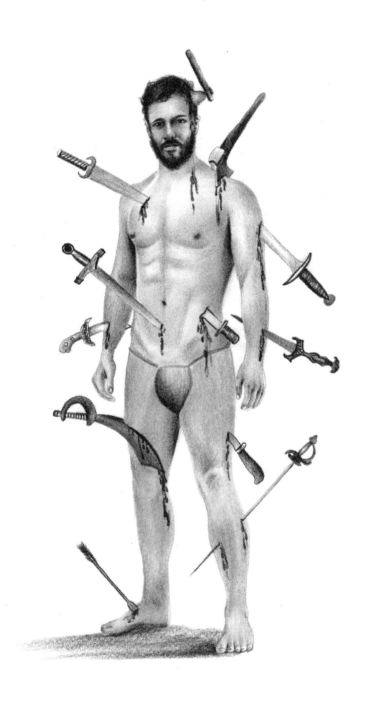

MEDIEVAL TORTURE AND EXECUTION
OF
MODERN SERIAL KILLERS

§

BILL DIEHR

Gore Galore Books

For my father, I hope I make you proud.

For my mother, may we one day find your killer

INTRODUCTION

Torment, for some men, is a need, an
appetite, and an accomplishment. —Emil
Cioran

W e have real-life monsters walking among us for whom we have a specific label: 'serial killers'. They may be much more common than anyone considers, yet they remain very much an enigma. Even with our modern age of infinitely expansive media channels, limits to human depravity seem to be non-existent.

FBI Behavioral Science Unit agent Robert Ressler coined the term "serial killer" in the 1970s. According to the FBI, a serial killer is someone who acts alone and who kills more than two people, with a cooling-off period of at least a month between the slayings. These people often derive enjoyment and even extreme pleasure in these exploits.

We hearken back to the malice of these horrifying crimes. However, does anyone ever want to know the motivating details behind them? I find the behind the scenes much more interesting than the common news articles, because that is where we will find the reasons why and how the person became what they are: hideous creatures from the most primitive depths of human nature.

It may never cross your mind, but there are countless people around us with horrible, dangerous personality disorders hidden beneath their external personas. These disorders are often brought about by a series of traumatic experiences and are in some cases simply caused by an unlucky draw of genetics. Most of the time, people are not even aware of the fact that they are standing right next to one of these creatures until it is too late.

At best, if you allow a person with this sickness close to you, the experience will eventually become a highly unpleasant one intermingled with a bit of emotional absurdity and a dash of wicked manipulation. Mix it in a shaker and you have yourself a toxic cocktail with a bitter spirit. At worst, it can lead to weeks or months of stalking, possible blackmail, and eventual kidnapping, subsequently leading to your murder.

It is the grisly, homicidal decisions which you will read about in this book that are the reason I so adamantly protest hitting and verbally abusing toddlers and children. The early years of a human's life are the absolute most important. When hitting and humiliating a child is used as a teaching practice or punishment, it shows the child that causing grief and physical pain to someone is an ordinary way of handling trivial situations. A victim of this upbringing will most likely carry on this behavior throughout their life, possibly developing sadistic personality disorder as a result. Many times, such a developed disposition for harassment will lie seemingly dormant until these victims enter into parenthood themselves. Mimicking their adolescent past, they will chastise their own children, not even realizing that they may be causing negative long-term effects on their children's psychological well-being and potentially causing emotional trauma.

For a toddler, such treatment creates confusion initiated by a misunderstanding of why they are being handled in this violent manner by someone who is supposed to protect and love them unconditionally, someone who they have put their undying trust in. This can be especially damaging considering that most of the time, young children and toddlers do not even know what they did wrong in the first place, and to a fragile mind these seemingly random violent responses have the potential to be irreparably demoralizing.

Are you for or against torture? I want you to think about it... Could you ever torture someone? Have you ever bullied, intimidated, beaten, threatened or intentionally humiliated anyone? These are the most overlooked and disregarded forms of torture of the modern world. Be it physical or psychological, the torment from having these inflicted upon you can be difficult to both recover from and refrain from doing to others. Could torture therefore be a way for humans to communicate the complicated feelings that they are incapable (or afraid) of articulating? What this says about human nature is a little disconcerting.

Although we no longer implement torture as capital punishment in most parts of the world, the sadistic implications of it being a long-time form of public entertainment are vivid in our culture. Why else are you compelled to read this type of literature? I liken it to a car accident...

When you hear the radio broadcaster say there is a collision just ahead on the same freeway that you are on, you get angry. Cursing at the radio, you ask why it has to be today. Why right now? Why, when you are already late for work? You are totally excusing the fact that someone may have been severely hurt or even killed a few hundred yards away. As you reduce to one lane, you rubberneck while slowly rolling by the site. In your animalistic, barbarous mind, unconscious curiosity prevails and you coldly eyeball the scene. You deeply want to see some metal-twisting carnage. The more devastating it appears, the more it encourages your interest. Even the average person can be cruel without saying a word or lifting a finger. American journalist Andy Rooney was right when he said, "The average dog is a nicer person than the average person."

In the first chapter of this book, I will discuss some of the personality disorders that lurk beneath the surface in both average people and serial killers. This information is important even if you are not dating a serial killer, because it's not just the serial killers among us who commit murder. In fact, you are more likely to be murdered by your lover if they are not a serial killer than if they are. Serial killers rarely kill people they know. This is because their approach to murder is a more logical one, and they understand that killing people they know is the easiest way to get caught. Emotionally unstable people, however, commit crimes of passion all the time, many seemingly wholly unprovoked. Thinking of someone who is excessively preoccupied with the reality that they could be stabbed to death in their sleep with a serrated steak knife by their spouse is kind of funny. I suppose that's what I'm looking to address.

First, I will be providing you with some brief explanations of these personality types so that you can get a decent grasp of what I am alluding to throughout the rest of the book. After that, we will delve into all the ghastly details as we explore some of the most horrendous serial killers in modern times. These animals ended the lives of many people in the most terrifying and disgusting ways while fervently enjoying every moment of it.

The thought experiment at the core of this book will be to explore which medieval torture and execution methods would have been implemented as punishment to each of these serial killers had they been convicted of their crimes in the dark ages. In my opinion, many would be well-deserved for such fiends. Whether you are for capital punishment or not, and considering it is a controversial topic, let us not overlook the victims. As the son of a murdered mother whose case has gone cold, I would want the most unbearable torture and execution possible performed on the person responsible. Obviously I am thinking by way of emotion when I say this. However, as I have admitted, even the average person can be cruel at times. Torturing a serial killer to death may seem barbaric, but so is cutting a woman's head off and using her windpipe as a sex toy. Moreover, did not the barbarians accept their fate on the battlefield? Regardless, I am not asking you to agree with my perspective, nor am I attempting to provoke you in any negative way. To be clear, I am not actually advocating that serial killers be tortured to death as current practice. My intent is purely to take you on a psychological journey into the horrific atrocities of human nature, both ancient and modern.

Is the current American prison system a place where criminals are reformed and come out changed for the better? Is it a punishment structure where criminals' network and think up new ways of not being caught? I think it can work in both ways and all ways for every kind of person. However, I truly believe that blatant, unremorseful, pleasure-seeking murder is unforgivable and deserving of equivalent retribution by means of capital punishment.

If you do not already, you may agree with me after reading this book. If you do agree with me, you might even change your mind. Either way, I want to make this reading experience as interesting and entertaining as I can make it. I have no malicious intent with this book, but it does come with a warning: these writings do not pander to the faint of heart or the easily offended.

Further, by envisioning what should have happened to these serial killers had they been convicted of their crimes in the dark ages, I intend to remind us of how refined our legal system actually is. Although it's not perfect, we have come far from the inhumane methods of torture and execution that were so enthusiastically and vehemently utilized by our pugnacious ancestors.

Although I do believe that there are good reasons for capital punishment, I also think there are more bad reasons than good. I wholeheartedly feel that hardened murderers should be the only people reserved for this treatment. Would the execution of these sadistic killers change what they did? Absolutely not. Regardless, as previously noted, this is a thought experiment, and it's ultimately up to you to decide if the crimes fit the punishments rendered in these pages.

This will not be an in-depth portrayal of each individual serial killer. I only intend to offer you the most interesting and damning bits, pertinent to their ultimate punishment and death, as I see fit. In addition, based on the individual, I am only privy to the information that they have allowed to be released through their confessions and the evidence gathered, so some chapters may be more detailed than others. If you are so inclined, you can easily satisfy your inquiring mind and indulge in the many great resources that I have utilized, which are listed at the end of this book. There are vast amounts of information made readily available through innumerable resources regarding these socially depraved, parasitic murderers. With so many interesting things to read, in fact, writing this book has itself been an enlightening and very rewarding experience.

Chapter 1

A Borderline, a Psychopath, and a Narcissist Walk into a Bar...

The healthy man does not torture others –
generally it is the tortured who turn into
torturers. —Carl Gustav Jung

In any discussion related to the extremes of human psychology, such as those about the most monstrous of serial killers, there are terms and concepts that regularly arise. I have researched such concepts, and while I remain no expert on personality disorders, through this research I have learned a substantial amount. With this in mind, I will establish these basic terms and definitions in order to offer you my conclusions. This way, you will know exactly my perspective as you read through each case.

The primary personality disorders you should be on the lookout for include the borderline, the psychopath, and the narcissist. Now, keep in mind that psychology is not perfect, and neither am I. There is much more that we do not know and are still actively pursuing understanding of. Essentially, psychology is identifying behaviors and habits and labeling them accordingly. Sigmund Freud once dominated psychology, yet a large amount of his studies have gone the way of the dodo bird. In this same way, I believe that much of modern psychology will become obsolete. Psychology is ever-changing, and many of what used to be known as "personality disorders" are no longer considered ailments. Although this is mainly societal, I am not stating that it is a good thing. I encourage you to keep this in mind as you continue through this book.

Further, psychology progresses as we learn more about human nature within this constant struggle that we cope with while living within ever-changing systems of community and communication. Not only is a new dynamic of dangerous habits and personalities emerging, but people also seem to be increasingly more apt to glorify them owing to the anonymity that many online forums provide. Try to name any disturbing fixation that could only exist inside a twisted mind, and there will be a thriving online community dedicated to it. Try to think of one right now. Child trafficking... recipes for cannibals... helping others commit suicide. Yes, they all exist.

It has been hotly debated, but I concede that most values and morality can be deliberated as social constructs depending on what era, country, or even what tribe we happen to inhabit. Good and bad, pious and evil, benevolent and malevolent, crazy and sane. These characteristics can have completely opposite meanings depending on the period and location of the society in which we live. Nevertheless, callous homicide is a universally identifiable criminal act worthy of equivalent reprisal. Some things are wrong no matter how you attempt to intellectually argue your way around it. Therefore, I do feel that objective morality exists, even if only in a few circumstances.

As far as we know, murder has always been an illicit act. It's not because people don't want to kill; actually, quite the opposite. Murder is unanimously criminal because people want to kill all the time. Whether a man stole another man's wife, or a boss fired someone for bad reasons, people have inner demons that they must battle in order to refrain from reacting violently. Hell, I want to kill someone nearly every night on my drive home from the office. Admittedly, whenever I am cut off as a vehicle races through traffic, I watch them recklessly swerve in and out of lanes, and I bitterly say aloud, "I hope you fucking die."

I am going off on a tangent here, but it's as if this particular stretch of highway has been hijacked by a modern-day Genghis Khan and his army of Mongol pillagers. Without fail, each night I have maniacs flipping me the bird and brake checking me for no good reason. That said, they probably hate the fact that I keep the fog-lights on while I drive.

Getting back to my point, the penalties for murder are intended to outweigh the incentives of murder, as they ought to. Further, the consequences must be extreme enough to effectively act as a deterrent for such behaviors. However, regardless of the penalty, these deterrents are not always good enough. Throughout civilized existence, even the likelihood of extreme and prolonged torture until death was not enough to prevent many people from carelessly killing one another. Most of the time, these acts can be attributed to extreme emotional distress or a range of personality disorders prevailing over consequential rationale.

One thing in particular that Sigmund Freud published that stands the test of time is the concept of the psychic apparatus. This explains that in the human mind, there are three main parts that contribute significantly to how we function in our day-to-day lives: the id, the ego, and the super ego.

The id is where our animal instinct comes from. This is also from where primitive emotions and feelings are derived. It is the part of the mind that needs to eat, fall in love, and is even where honesty comes from. The id does not plan. It can only feel what it feels in the moment. Further, these instinctual impulses and emotions are consciously uncontrollable.

The ego is derived from the more logical, intuitive, and scientific side of the brain. However, neither the ego nor the id is necessarily rational, and to balance the two halves we have the super ego, which is the "self" part of the brain. The super ego observes the mental processes and rationalizes between the contending halves. It has been noted that in serial killers, it appears that the super ego part of the brain is either flawed or hardly present at all. These people go sashaying around, leaving devastating consequences in their wake in nearly every facet of life.

This is the main difference between a sane person and an insane person. The sane have healthy super egos which help to balance the mind, and the insane rely on animal instinct and self-gratifying impulses to muster fulfillment as they live out their tragic existences. This may not be a politically correct explanation of someone with a mental disorder. However, as history confirms, the actions performed by these sadistic lunatics serve no purpose in a world that so many have selflessly sacrificed their lives to preserve.

The Borderline

Borderline personality disorder is quite difficult to explain. Many psychologists even have a hard time explaining it. Borderlines can be some of the biggest assholes out there, but also some of the sweetest people you will get to meet. However, some have the potential to be extremely dangerous to have in your life since their true motives can easily go unnoticed. I hope I do a good job informing you, because I have crossed paths with a couple of borderline monstrosities before, and it was, to say the least, quite unpleasant.

The borderline is essentially a perversion of the phlegmatic personality type. The phlegmatic is an introverted person, yet very much a people person. Phlegmatic personality types go along with the scene around them, are not provocative, and enjoy the company of other people. They go to where many people congregate but will not initiate conversation. However, the phlegmatic has a super ego that tends to balance out the id and the ego, so they tend not to be dangerous individuals.

The borderline is, for the most part, pure id with virtually no super ego. A mantra that one with this personality disorder might live by would sound something like, "You're either the butcher or the cattle." Does your lover have a saying that sounds similar to this? They are a whirlwind of love, hate, pleasure, pain, and depression, with no anchor.

The borderline is hardly an extrovert and will barely ever approach others. However, they need other people to either approach them or at least notice them. A way that many bait themselves is to go to a populated place like a bar or café and sit alone with a book in their hand with the intention of attracting others. They will be reading something that they are scarcely interested in and will likely never finish. They will usually be reading somewhere in the beginning of the book. The title will have a topic that they want people to attribute to them based on whatever their artificial character happens to be that day, week, or month. Another way they lure people is with their style of hair or clothing. Many of them will take on a particular trend and try to manifest a personality typical to that style. With that, they may constantly change their ethics and ideals based on each conversation that they are engaged in, trying to hook others. However, be aware that this is not common in all borderlines, just ones with anti-social tendencies or clandestine motives. Although this isn't the classic borderline, it is exactly the type that you should be mindful of. Luckily, they are easy to sniff out after a five-minute conversation. On the other hand, you could simply point them out as the guy wearing the cowboy hat, or the girl wearing non-prescription black-framed glasses, or it could be the person wearing a scarf in the summer. This of course applies to everyone except my readers. You are clearly superior and are never wrong or disingenuous, and you can do whatever you want. Do not be afraid to tell that to everyone who approaches you at the café today as you read this with your hip glasses on.

Returning, the ego in the borderline is majorly consumed by the id, which is the source of their craving for attention. The borderline may not even care what type of attention it gets, so long as it gets some. It will take a beating and humiliation; it will take anything, so long as it is getting the attention that it craves. They are an unbiased glutton for attention, an addict, if you will. When actually harmed, they will utilize that victimization as a method for further attention seeking. Although they may not have preferred the abuse, they will not let it go to waste. As stated by politician Rahm Emanuel, "You never let a serious crisis go to waste. What I mean by that is it's an opportunity to do things you think you could not do before."

The borderline is not necessarily the initiator of violence. They espouse the victim of violence. However, this does not mean that they will not kill. When they do, they again assume the role of the victim. While either facing the consequences or explaining the reasons for their actions, they will often blame their own victims for driving them to murder. They commonly adopt the role of the bullied and severely abused whose hands were forced by means of "self-defense."

Be it mentally or physically (or both), they often incur much of the abuse upon themselves in a twisted sort of way. They demand this attention to fulfill the voracious appetite of their id. I personally believe that this is how masochism is derived. I presume borderline personality disorder and masochism have a direct symbiotic correlation, and without it, masochism may otherwise be nonexistent.

I conclude this section by reiterating that of these three personality disorders, it is my opinion that this one has the highest potential for danger. I advise people to be extremely careful and aware of the consequences if they have someone in their life who exhibits much of this behavior. Taking a person like this out of your life can be very difficult, because you may be afraid to do so. Take it from me, it's not easy to break up with someone who threatens to kill themselves and make it look like you did it. The best thing to do is ignore their behavior and do not allow them to elicit a response from you. Eventually, they will get bored, and when they have a new victim on their radar, they will shift their focus to that next target. This is how I was passively able to remove myself from a destructive relationship with an unstable borderline with extreme mood swings and violent tendencies.

The Psychopath

Right off the bat, I should address the fact that most psychopaths are not violent. Regardless, many of them can be if they believe it serves a higher purpose, or if they are of the sadistic type, which is also not that common. As of now, we may not know the absolute causes of psychopathy. However, it is typically believed to be a combination of a genetic dysfunction and negative childhood environmental factors, such as poor parenting. To expand, being genetically predisposed to psychopathy does not mean that one will have the symptoms of being a psychopath. Nearly all full-blown psychopaths come from broken homes and/or chronic abusive interpersonal relationships.

Contrary to popular belief, one does not have to suffer from any type of antisocial personality disorder in order to be a serial killer. Instead, they can kill with no reservations or conscience due to their ability to adapt as social people; through compartmentalization, they dehumanize their victims. This is how they are able to function unsuspected. Their common encounters are not conflated with their desire to murder. Only when they have a victim in mind is that compulsion valued and pursued. The serial killer partitions everyone else in their life from the victim. They want to kill for the thrill and entertainment that they receive from either the act of it or what they do afterward. Their morals are not an issue for them. They kill because it is fun and/or sexually satisfying to them. This is sadistic, and virtually anyone could have this sort of mentality. However, most experts agree that most serial killers are sociopaths or psychopaths.

What commonly describes someone with psychopathic symptoms is a complete lack of empathy. However, lack of empathy is common among many people within so many professional environments that it would not make sense to define a person as a psychopath unless they exhibited the perfect storm of additional symptoms. The trio is complete when a person creates false presentations of their self and compartmentalizes & dehumanizes people while having a complete lack of empathy. Regardless, this person may not necessarily be described as a psychopath just because they exhibit callous behavior, as the CEO of a multi-national corporation might, for example. The CEO may use this behavior as an asset to be utilized for difficult decision-making for the greater good of the company. However, your local dogcatcher who goes around acting cold and cruel with no purpose other than to embellish their ego may be reasonably defined as a full-blown psychopath. These are the most unpleasant people, whom you should never hope to meet.

It has been discovered that there is a disproportionate number of psychopath CEO's relative to any other occupation. However, professional aspirations may placate their dominance and ruthlessness. With this, their psychopathy is absorbed by cutthroat business dealings rather than torment and murder. This can ultimately give them an edge in a world that may otherwise have emotional consequences based on questionable actions. Whether the difficult decisions that they must make come out with positive or negative effects on others involved, the choice has been made through a purely logical method. Concerning this, they may have complete disbelief in the concept of moral dilemmas altogether. One character I always think of that could rightly be misinterpreted as this personality type is Star Trek's Spock. Among so many memorable quotes that distinguish him from human beings, my favorite is, "May I say that I have not thoroughly enjoyed serving with humans? I find their illogic and foolish emotions a constant irritant." As unlikely as it is, this leads me to question whether or not Spock was a psychopath.

Another major characteristic that describes a psychopath is a general lack of ability to discern right from wrong, usually morally or legally (or both). They tend not to care for morals or values, yet they may incongruently recognize them with maturity, or at least act like it when their deplorable actions become known. It's as if the serial killers who are afflicted with this ailment have zero self-awareness, until magically they are apprehended, and society labels them a monster. Only then will they explain how remorseful they are, how they could not control themselves. I say they are lying. I truly think they are saying these things in order to manipulate others. For example, some people have bizarre impulses to masturbate in public places, such as on trains and busses. The vast majority of these people do not do it. However, the few that do sure are sorry after being caught and placed on a sex offenders list. They will apologize to their grave, but they are not actually sorry. They are only sorry that they got caught. This is the same with serial killers. Most of the time, they are sexually motivated to do these inherently evil crimes. However, there are likely innumerable people around us who have these same sadistic impulses and perversions yet choose not to act on them. Further, the excuse that they had no self-awareness while they were in their murderous heyday is falsified by the fact that they must have extreme self-awareness to develop skillful impression management. This ability must be mastered in order to successfully lure their victims in the first place. Impression management is the act of taking on an enticing persona in order to elicit a specific response from the intended party. To do this effectively, you must have great control regulating your own actions and responses in social interactions. Ted Bundy, in particular, was a master of deception in the way of creating characters that required the assistance of anyone on the street. When someone like that says they had no control over themselves, and they didn't know what they were doing until after the fact, they're basically full of shit, in my opinion.

I am going to go off on another tangent here and say that I find it incredibly interesting how our minds work to exchange regret for sympathy. For example, consider a total social parasite; they habitually lie, cheat, and steal. Yet they will always materialize some excuse for why they do what they do as a means to justify their debauchery. They know that they are scumbags, yet they will go to exhausting lengths in attempts to preserve their public image. Rarely are these people honest and willing to admit that they are gigantic pieces of shit. You will practically never hear them utter, "What can I say? I'm a terrible person." Even with killers facing the death penalty, it is as if they need people to believe that they are either innocent or a victim. To the fitting of the noose, they will attempt to either justify their actions or claim remorse. Seldom will they refrain from trying to change the perceptions of their critics. It is as if human nature is predisposed to require social acceptance under every circumstance, no matter how futile it is. In fact, many serial killers have tried to claim victimization while awaiting their death sentence. Bundy, for example, tried to blame violent pornography for his sadistic necrophilia urges. H. H. Holmes tried to recant his written confession, dramatically reducing his number of victims to only two. They compulsively seek societal tolerance, reaching out their hands in a last-ditch effort for what... something to hold on to? It is like drowning to death, impulsively taking your last gasp for air while underwater.

To get back to the topic at hand, psychopaths often tend to challenge common rules and laws unless it serves their own personal interests. They also seem to have an inflated sense of self-worth and are priggishly callous with an inability to put themselves in other peoples' shoes. A psychopath is practically incapable of experiencing feelings of guilt, shame, or embarrassment. As Kyle Reese says in the movie *"The Terminator" (1984)*, "It can't be bargained with. It can't be reasoned with. It doesn't feel pity, or remorse, or fear. And it absolutely will not stop, ever, until you are dead."

At the very least, they are quite petty, and may simply steal your wallet, purse, or any other valuables accessible to them. A lot of them become shoddy, rinky-dink salesmen and will attempt to sell you worthless rubbish that you have no use for. Yet they will go to embarrassing lengths in attempts to convince you that you need what they are selling.

In other cases, many of them get into law enforcement, politics, or even enter the corporate business world with aspirations of global dominance (no matter how insignificant their goals are). Imagine a middle-aged help desk operator who believes that they will become the CEO of Microsoft. Even after many years of never advancing past the call center, he will be the model employee for as long as his irrational mind believes that he is destined for greatness. Think Dwight Schrute from the television show *"The Office"*. A bizarre paper salesperson whose sole aspiration in life is to be the floor manager. Personally, I think he is one of the funniest characters of all time. A perfect quote to illustrate my point on the corporate psychopath is when he said, "Nothing stresses me out. Except having to seek the approval of my inferiors."

When these psychopaths' dreams are eventually crushed and they are somehow made aware of their foolhardiness, bad things can and most likely will happen. This type of psychopath may never accept the reality of mediocrity. Once this occurs, they will create some way to justify a very new behavior, be it ethical or not (according to our standards). One case, in particular, that parallels this scenario is that of United States Postal Service worker Patrick Sherrill. In August of 1986, after being reprimanded by management and facing possible termination, Patrick walked in to work the next day brandishing two pistols. Without prejudice, he killed fourteen coworkers and injured six more before blasting himself in the forehead. This event is what inspired the macabre term, "going postal."

Controversially, we frequently see detestable behavior in America with an overwhelming number of police brutality cases. Heavy-fisted adrenaline addicts justifying violent tactics through a falsified greater good self-perception. It is an unfortunate reality that psychopathy runs rampant in law enforcement. Isn't that a little unsettling? Armed people employed to enforce the same laws that they have neither respect nor concern for... Again, this of course only applies to those who are not currently reading this book.

At worst, a psychopath can be an evil, sadistic monstrosity that will torment you to get what they want. They will have no problem with using physical force, or even murder, to achieve their selfish desires. Once detected, these are the ones who can be very dangerous and should be avoided, even if it means losing other relationships in the process.

The Narcissist

Psychopathy is widespread within government, large corporations, and law enforcement. While borderline personality disorder appears to run rampant with every other stranger. Narcissism, too, is endemic to our current culture. For the past few decades, we have been living in a "me me me, look how God-damned special I am" type of society. Now we are left with this dystopian internet sub-culture craving their detached practice of attention-seeking via social media websites.

Taking a trip in a time machine and peering out at another world from fifty years ago, one could easily assume that narcissism was a part of everyday life for the common person of the future. You would be perfectly reasonable to conclude that self-absorption is an adapted behavior in this stage of humanity. Regarding this, I wonder whether this is a new phenomenon or if people have been this way since before the advent of social media. Further, if they were, how did they ever find their release? Certainly, fifty years ago, the common housewife wasn't telephoning her entire circle of friends and relatives for the sole reason of complaining about how long the line at the grocery store was.

Moreover, it is hard for me to understand the fascination that the masses have with these reality shows that endorse certain behavioral flaws as celebrity-worthy attributes. Yet these television programs have become very popular these days. Therefore, it is safe to assume that these distinct personality disorders are copiously celebrated. Need I say that this does not contribute much to our cultural evolution? However, humor comes in many forms, and we would be right to mock one who acts like a fool. This is not what is occurring. These celebrity jesters are inundated with riches and fame rather than being clad with a much-warranted dunce hat, striped tights, and pointy shoes with bells on the toes.

With that in consideration, there is an absolute distinction between behaving like a narcissist and actually being a clinically diagnosed narcissist. A good example of common narcissistic behavior is the wannabe fashion diva who portrays herself as a famous model. In actuality, she wears bootleg clothing and works a menial job while submitting to older men for money and gifts in exchange for time and sexual favors. There's also the arrogant bodybuilder who prides himself as an Adonis. He is a Casanova who thinks that every glance in his direction from both males and females is a sign that he is desired sexually. Regardless, these people are more annoying than they are dangerous, and they are usually quite harmless.

Nevertheless, like the psychopath, some very dangerous narcissists out there will inflict emotional havoc on you. They may possibly even kill given the perfect storm of distress. Even so, they tend to be quite simple-minded people. Whenever I think of a narcissist, I think of the ancient kings, queens, and pharaohs who had peasants massaging their feet, waving fans, and feeding them grapes as the glorious one lay atop a bed of exotic flower petals.

The narcissist lives to be worshipped. They need to be acknowledged as the biggest badass in the room, the hottest girl at the bar, or the funniest guy at the party. This is whatever their self-perceived essence happens to be. They tend to be extremely extroverted, and at any given chance, they will often chastise others if they perceive them as a threat. Additionally, they will often use their powers of influence to turn others against that threat, ultimately doing whatever they can to ensure that the target will not have the opportunity to surpass them in any way (be it socially or professionally). This especially applies to workplace environments and within circles of friends.

Another example of this dysfunctional personality type is the person who is constantly inclined to advocate some healthy lifestyle that they "have been living for years." However, if it is a lifestyle that they are not an expert in, when questioned and probed about it they will invent a contrarian viewpoint that corresponds with their claims. For instance, if you are either a doctor or dietitian, then they will find some new-fangled fab diet and claim to be some type of "expert" on Chinese Herbal Healing or whatever. They will completely discount your entire field of knowledge which you have spent your life's work studying. A humble, sane person can admit when they are wrong, choosing not to espouse lies simply to create a falsely superior image of themselves to the uninformed. Nonetheless, too many ignorant people fall victim to these half-wit swindlers.

The narcissist often seeks to intimidate and bully their opposition (or perceived opposition). They want to intimidate them in the hopes that they will either fold or follow and worship them, ultimately breaking their spirit into giving in. This happens in the workplace all too often. Narcissists want to be the center of attention, the focal point of the story. They are the protagonist that desperately needs other people to take part in their play. Regardless, every now and then reality springs into action, exposing the narcissist for what they are. This will sabotage the narcissists' illusion, devastating the fantasy world that they so meticulously developed. When this happens, it is referred to as a narcissistic reset.

The narcissist will not face the reality of merely being an average person. This is often what happens when you see once famous artists going indie or solo, playing at small venues and in smoky basements. They may say things like "bands aren't what a true musician does" or "a true musician doesn't submit their art to just anybody." They constantly reinterpret the world around them to make themselves the arbiter of their own relativity.

When their plans fall through, they will say, "I meant to do that," never humbling themselves and growing from their failures. Ironically, they are habitually inclined to justify why they failed as a conscious decision to "humble" themselves. Then something else happens... When the narcissist's self-esteem is eventually destroyed, and they can no longer create a narrative that warps the reality of those around them, they fall into a narcissistic rage.

A narcissistic rage happens when the narcissist unleashes their anger and frustration on everyone and everything around them. The inevitable trigger can happen anytime, and it can make the narcissist extremely aggressive and violent, possibly driving them to commit murder or suicide or both. Because these acts of rage are emotionally charged and hardly ever planned, this could be a good enough reason not to spend copious amounts of time with these types of people. The reason being that literally anyone and everyone could be perceived as the reason for their decline in life. If the narcissist believes that their reputation has been irreparably tarnished, not even their closest of friends is safe.

Luka Magnotta, the gay porn star who produced the infamous viral video "1 Lunatic 1 Ice Pick," is the posterchild for the sadistic narcissist. In May 2012, he filmed himself killing thirty-four-year-old international student Lin Jun. The video showed Jun tied to a bed frame with Luka standing over him, stabbing him with an ice pick and knife. While filming himself dismembering Jun's lifeless body, Luka jokingly detached an arm and masturbated with it. Then he crawled on top of Jun's headless corpse and had sex with it. Once he was finished, Luka packaged various mutilated body parts and sent them all over Canada. He even had the nerve to send the left foot and right hand to a couple of elementary schools in Vancouver.

Luka did it for the fame. As a failed male model and rejected reality TV show applicant, his sick and selfish mind led him to conjure up the most depraved way that he could undoubtedly obtain recognition. With an exaggerated grandeur about himself, along with an indifferent feeling for others, Luka did this with a complete lack of moral reservation. Make no mistake, Luka was a textbook narcissist. In an uncomfortable moment during an interview with a reality television show producer, he bizarrely stated, "I've been told that I'm devastatingly good looking," and was followed by an awkward silence. Of course, he was not chosen to be on the show.

Consequently, Luka gained the infamy that he desperately desired. After fleeing Canada, he soon got a front cover feature on Interpol's 'Red Notice' list, prompting an international manhunt. He was caught a month later in Berlin. During the trial, multiple psychological experts diagnosed him as having both narcissistic and borderline personality disorder. In the end, Luka was found guilty and received life in prison, with the possibility of parole in 25 years. Therefore, he could be a free man by the age of 55. That being the case, Canada is rather lenient on their convicted murderers. Prior to the abolishment of capital punishment in 1963, Canada's only method of execution was death by hanging.

Chapter 2

Causality

To me, this world is nothing but evil, and
my own evil just happened to come out
'cause of the circumstances of what I was
doing. —Aileen Wuornos

The FBI defines causality as "a complex process based on biological, social, and environmental factors." They go on to explain that each individual chooses how they will engage in certain behaviors. The way people mentally absorb and habituate their experiences and surroundings will determine their future self.

Somewhere along the line, serial killers have twisted their sense of morality due to whatever mental perversions prevailed. To be specific on the precise causes of serial killer behavior is just as impossible as specifying the causes of normal behavior. One cannot use a broad brush to paint an explanation of serial killers' conduct. Each case is as different as it is for anyone who commits any other type of crime. Motives and objectives are only to be determined by the killer, for the killer. We observers cannot be sure of anything. We only know what killers lead us to believe through their words, actions, and other peoples' experiences with them. Considering their record, nothing is fully believable when it is directly expressed by a serial killer.

When attempting to determine causality, we must look into the major events in a killer's life that have a direct correlation with their future behavior. That's why we should look at each case individually. The FBI states, "The development of social coping mechanisms begins early in life and continues to progress as children learn to interact, negotiate, and compromise with their peers. In some individuals, the failure to develop adequate coping mechanisms results in violent behavior." Throughout the process of researching for this book, if I have discovered any relevant material about a serial killer's past, it will be used to outline a basic connection to their future behavior within each chapter. For myself, I attempt to establish some degree of logic as to how a person could possibly enjoy harming innocent people. However, as someone who is not afflicted with sociopathy, I may never truly understand.

To better recognize them, serial killers' motives have been greatly researched and explored. Although have some of the greatest minds of our time working on creating a comprehensible profile of such deranged people, it has nonetheless proven to be a formidable task. This is because profiling a typical serial killer is tantamount to profiling someone who practices autoerotic asphyxiation. There is not a serial killer 'type'. This is why, whenever these people are discovered, it's such a shock to their friends and family. Edmund Kemper, for instance, regularly drank with off-duty police officers at his local bar. He unassumingly discussed the investigation of himself with them even while the body of a young girl was in the trunk of his car. Kemper was often referred to as a "gentle giant."

As of 2014, there were as many as 25 known serial killers actively operating in the United States, with a total of 45 operating between 2010 and 2014. However, those statistics only cover those that have been caught. You should expect there to be many times more out there. According to the Radford University/FGCU Serial Killer Database, the top three motives for murder are enjoyment (thrill, lust, power), financial gain, and anger. For some reason, the United States is especially burdened with an epidemic of serial killers. America tops the charts with 2,743 total known serial killers. This towers over England's distant second place, which has only 145. At any time in the United States, the FBI estimates that there are 30 to 35 serial killers currently stalking their victims. So, in the words of animator Trey Parker, creator of South Park, "Freedom isn't free. Now there's a hefty fuckin' fee."

Serial killers have been categorized into three different types: the visionary, the missionary, and the hedonist. Although many fall under a single category, some will assume more than one, or even all of them at different points throughout their killing career. As people normally do, serial killers change their preferences and habits with age. Motives, practices, and behaviors will often reflect a certain degree of change as one matures while living with this deadly complex. Some serial killers may change their method of murder so much that they could potentially be assumed as two or more completely different killers over a period of time. Although it makes sense for them to do this purposefully, there is no way of telling what catalyzes their change in tactics.

Visionaries

Visionaries are, to put it plainly, the full-blown crazy ones. Basically, they hear voices in their heads. Some are also motivated by erroneous visions, like seeing the bust of Jesus Christ in wood grain. These delusions may be interpreted as a higher power giving them specific instructions for murder. It's tough to imagine someone thinking, "Oh look, it's an image of God hanging out on the bathroom door. Looks like I'm going to have to sacrifice an infant and rape the neighbor's dog." However, some sick bastard has or will have that exact thought under the right circumstances.

Personally, I think people try to find meaning in meaningless things. They want to think that they are more important than they actually are, so they are subconsciously looking for "signs" from a spiritual realm. Further, I think people have a natural tendency to attribute coincidences to something greater than themselves. Like having a dream about a plane crash a week before seeing a news report about the same kind of incident. Now this person thinks that they had an otherworldly vision. All of a sudden, they are an incarnation of Silvia Browne. Even to a highly intelligent mind, this can easily happen. It actually does happen all the time. It is not a huge stretch to think that a string of coincidences could lead an anti-social zealot to believe that a God is instructing them to kill through messages that only they have the ability to see and interpret.

Missionaries

Missionaries are killers who think that they are doing the greater good of society by ridding it of a certain group of people. They often target prostitutes or members of a particular ethnic background. It isn't difficult to picture what kind of person they must be in their daily life. I imagine a self-righteous bravado, aggressively criticizing a woman for breast feeding her baby in public. However, it's more likely a mild-mannered guy crunching numbers in a cubicle.

To put it plainly, the missionary killer is the typical character we see on popular television shows like "Dexter". A hip, forensic technician who quenches his thirst to kill by slaying uncaptured murderers. This kind of serial killer is often celebrated, and their mental disorders are glorified as they are shrouded in a plot riddled with ethical dilemmas. However, reality is not as glamorous. Much of the time, a missionary serial killer is targeting the very thing that they are guilty of themselves. For instance, they may pick up a prostitute, rape or have sex with her, then strangle her to death for being a whore. Another might kill a kid for being gay but then masturbate on his face.

Hedonists

Hedonists are the most common type of serial killer. They are traditionally referred to as "thrill seekers." These fiends get off on the act of harming others. Typically, their motives are lust, power, and personal gain.

Lust is a very common element in some of the more disturbing murder scenes. It seems like whenever sex is involved, shit gets weird. You will see cases where a killer has sex with a decaying corpse to the point of requiring tweezers to pull maggots out of his dick. The late George Carlin summed it up best by saying, "Animals don't fuck their dead. A rat will do a lot of gross things, but he will not fuck a dead rat. It wouldn't even occur to him. Only a human being would think to fuck someone who just died."

Killers who commit murder for personal gain are typically motivated by social or financial benefit. These serial killers could come from any range of classes or households. The lower class petty killer may pick out a wealthy looking couple to mug. They may kill out of a mix of ease and cowardice in retrieving the money from their victim. In some situations, it's easier to pull a wallet from a dead man than from a living one. Their initial intent may not be to kill, but they will if they believe that they are no longer in control of the situation. This is why if you're ever being mugged, it's best to give up your wallet and live to fight another day.

Another circumstance in which a serial killer may have something to gain is when killing off their competition in the workplace. This would be a very ruthless businessman type. He would likely come from a middle- to upper-class household. However, he would not be the type to be afraid to get his hands dirty. The kind of character I imagine is a flannel-wearing son of a sawmill lumber supplier who feels shafted for not being promoted to CEO of the company.

Power seekers are those who kill for the God-like feeling that they get by being the arbiter of their victim's fate. A textbook example of this kind of killer is Dennis Rader, otherwise known as the BTK killer. He was a sad man with a boring life who was as narcissistic as they come. Being a complete loser, he hardly had control over his own life, let alone anybody else's. Only when he finally got his dream job, as a dogcatcher and compliance manager, was he able to fill that need for power over others. Once this happened, he took a long hiatus from killing.

With these typologies in mind, I wonder if there is another kind of killer out there. One so outlandish and unconventional that their motivations may never be uncovered. Hypothetically, I could believe that there is a certain brand of serial killer who has existed for as long as civilized man has. This is the kind of killer who is so efficient and undetectable that their existence will neither be discovered, nor suspected. This kind of person could be the slickest son of a bitch you've never heard of.

Of course, we know that this type of person can exist. I compare it to video games with world-wide leaderboards. You could dedicate your entire summer to this certain video game, playing for up to 18 hours a day. Regardless, you may never even reach the top 1000 rankings. You sit back in utter defeat and wonder how someone could be so goddamned good at this game. You can't even imagine how a score that high could possibly be obtained. Even if you were to watch the first-place player achieve their score, you would marvel in disbelief. Even seeing it firsthand, you couldn't fathom how a human being could achieve such perfection. Now imagine that this 'best in the world' player is instead engaged in their own reality game of serial murder. Under every circumstance, for everything in life, there must be a "best of," or in this case, "worst of."

This type of imperceptible serial killers' motives may not fall under any category. They may be so corrupt that they thought serial murder would be a challenging undertaking. Similar to gaming, they may not receive any gratuitous amount of thrill or joy from their exploits. They want to hone their skills to perfection. They aspire to be the best, obtain the highest score, and never leave a trace. They operate so quickly and seamlessly that they are nearly impossible to detect. Each movement is meticulously performed with absolute precision. Every single action, from stalking to killing, is done flawlessly. If you were able to view it, this would be a sight to behold. It would be mind boggling to know that someone is able to think and maneuver with such excellence. Because they would not have any sexual or mental partialities connected with the act of killing, they would be much less likely to make the same mistakes that others less fortunate inevitably do. Further, to ensure their continued success and elusiveness, they would always leave the crime scene to appear as if the death of their victims was either natural or performed in such a way that the murder would be irrefutably pinned on another individual, such as a family member or spouse.

Thinking about convicted murderers who claim innocence until death, a small part of me wonders if this scenario may have occurred. Also, I tend to wonder if so many mysterious cases in history, such as 'spontaneous human combustion' (SHC), were a result of this type of serial killer. A kind of expert who left the world befuddled with ridiculous explanations. There is currently no understanding of what the cause of SHC is. It is described as death by a fire with no external source. However, the claim that a fire could be ignited inside a living human body is quite unsubstantiated.

In a similar way, the bizarre death of Canadian tourist Elisa Lam could be another case that defies rationale, unless you imagine a killer such as this to be responsible. Elisa Lam's body was discovered on February 19, 2013, after residents of the Cecil Hotel in Los Angeles complained about a black sludge being present in their tap water. She was found inside the hotel's giant water tank, located on the roof. The black sludge that they were drinking was her decomposing body. The strange part is that the security footage shows Elisa frantically pressing elevator floor buttons, making bizarre hand gestures and appearing to be hiding from someone who was not captured on video. It is also a mystery how she was able to both gain access to the roof without activating any alarms and get inside the tank by opening and closing the heavy lid by herself. Her baffling death was ruled "accidental drowning."

To be honest, I hope to God that killers like this don't exist. However, the more that I think about it, the more plausible they seem. If a person like this is not out there right now, they most likely have been, or will be. Possibly even coming to a town near you.

Chapter 3

A Brief History of Torture and Punishment

Turning the weapons of the enemy against
him is, of course, of grave danger to one's
soul. It is nonetheless a satisfying thing to
see. —Inquisitor Havelock Brundsted

From forcing someone to drink water until they are violently ill and bloated to burning someone's armpits until their innards are visible, torture has been a part of mankind for as long as people have been able to communicate. As we've already accepted, most people are pretty terrible to begin with. The basic need for prehistoric man to formulate rules to restrict cruelty from occurring within their tribes is a direct insight into our inherent malice. To make it worse, place these savages in a feudal civilization where life is bleak, harsh, and unforgiving. When the substantial majority exhibit severe religious intolerance and a complete lack of education, you have yourself a downright cruel and vicious society. Mind you, primitive men and women are no different than the people of today. If you could pluck any infant from medieval Europe and raise it in today's world, you wouldn't notice a difference. This works both ways. Raise a modern child in Medieval Europe and in no time, it will be looking forward to the next public execution the same as one waits for their favorite television show to release a new episode today.

There have been many definitions of torture throughout the years. However, many of those definitions rule out lawful sanctions and incarceration facilities. If we are to follow most definitions, individuals working under some government capacities may have certain exceptions to the rule. Specifically, I believe it is torture for prison conditions to be so appalling that it is hazardous and/or toxic to the health of its denizens. Although no one person may be directly performing the torture, it is a reflection of deliberate circumstance. Currently not as common, death due to imprisonment was an ordinary occurrence in the 1700s. Around 1 in 4 prisoners died from their living conditions, stripped of all necessities. I think that forcing someone to live in a brick box with no bedding, heat, or toilet should be defined as torture.

With that in mind and for these works, I respect the 1975 *Declaration of Tokyo* definition, as adopted by the World Medical Assembly. I believe it to be the most reasonable, official definition. It states, "...torture is defined as the deliberate, systematic, or wanton infliction of physical or mental suffering by one or more persons acting alone or on the orders of any authority, to force another person to yield information, to make a confession, or for any other reason."

Torturous Tyrants

Torture has been universally legal for around 3000 years. The earliest recorded account was that of the Egyptians under pharaoh Ramses II, regarding the Battle of Kadesh in 1274 BC. Noted as one of the most well-documented battles from ancient times, it was a massive demonstration of brutality and human cruelty between Egypt and the Hittite Empire (modern-day Turkey).

A couple of Shasu spies on the side of the Hittite army were captured and roughed up by Egyptian scouts. From an ancient carving depicting the torture performed to get information pertaining to the location of the Hittite army, it appears the spies were caned by a crowd of Egyptian militiamen. After this, they revealed the location and readiness of the opposing army. The information obtained was crucial for Ramses II's survival in the battle, since a poor strategy had initially been planned using misinformation given by other unsuspected Hittite infiltrators. Although vastly outnumbered, the newly acquired information allowed for the Egyptian army to have a fighting chance. To this day, it is a hotly debated topic who was the ultimate victor.

The earliest known culture to implement systematic torture and execution practices were the ancient Assyrians, starting around the 14th century BC. This was mostly done for military reasons in order to frighten their adversaries into submission. These people were very proud of their tactics; so proud, in fact, that they typically used the skulls of their enemies as lawn and tree ornaments. This makes sense, considering that they employed head hunters to scrounge about sacked cities and cut the heads off of corpses to be taken back to a scribe to be tallied. These heads must have been an embarrassment of riches, considering their conquests. Further, engravings suggest that the Assyrians also impaled naked prisoners of war after their invasion of Judah in 701 BC. This practice continued regularly to warn others of the consequences of noncompliance. If a city refused to surrender immediately, many of its citizens were impaled right outside the city walls. Under the rule of King Ashurnasirpal, he had an entire city massacred and the nobles flayed alive, removing the skin from their entire bodies. They draped the skin atop mountains of carcasses, and hung them from castle walls. It didn't end there; sometimes, the skins of their enemies were used as decorative covers for furniture. Other times, captured enemies were mutilated. Arms, hands, ears, and noses were cut off. Some were blinded with hot branding irons, others brained with a mace, and the rest, decapitated. In medieval times, if you were in the line to be beheaded, you would be grateful for small blessings. It also doesn't appear as if the Assyrian kings were in the slightest perturbed as to the morality of massacring thousands of innocent civilians. King Sennacherib proudly describes a massacre in a sort of sadistic way that we only expect a serial killer to. In an uncovered ancient inscription, he states:

"With the weapons of [the god] Assur, my lord, and the terrible onset of my attack, I stopped their advance, I succeeded in surrounding them [or turning back], I decimated the enemy host with arrow and spear. All of their bodies I bore through like a sieve... Speedily I cut them down and established their defeat. I cut their throats like lambs. I cut off their precious lives [as one cuts] a string. Like the many waters of a storm, I made [the contents of] their gullets and entrails run down upon the wide earth. My prancing steeds, harnessed for my riding, plunged into the streams of their blood as [into] a river. The wheels of my war chariot, which brings low the wicked and the evil, were bespattered with blood and filth. With the bodies of their warriors I filled the plain, like their belts, and seized the girdled daggers of gold and silver which [they carried] on their persons."

It would be horrifying for a leader today to describe a modern battle in this way. The world would rightly perceive that person as a threat to humanity. However, this was commonplace in ancient times. Kings regularly gave themselves more credit than they deserved. With their own narratives, they placed themselves on the front line, heroically slaughtering their adversaries in an epic demonstration of might.

To be expected, prisoners of war were treated particularly cruelly by our ancestors. However, it was considered virtuous to refrain from callous torture and murder of innocent captured enemies. This was apparent when, in an unprecedented event, Carthaginian prisoners were handed over to the widow of a recently killed Roman statesman, Marcus Atilius Regulus, in 250 BC. The widow, Marcia, killed the prisoners in the same way that Marcus Regulus was killed. There are various accounts of what actually happened to him, but the consensus is that his eyelids were either cut off or sewn into his face, and he was exposed to the grueling mid-day sun, after which he was placed inside a barrel that was lined with iron spikes. They rolled him down a hill and left him there to die. Regulus was revered as a hero, and for only this reason was his wife allowed by Senate to exact her revenge on prisoners whom had nothing to do with his death. This sparked much debate among the scholars of their time. These debates help us to understand that the notion of justifiable torture was not undisputed.

Throughout ancient history, many tyrants have offered us an unusual glimpse of human cruelty. It's chillingly expected that when you give a man infinite power over others and their environment, he becomes a sadistic monster. Put that man in a barbaric time when life is as cheap as a loaf of bread, and you get to see the endless lengths of human depravity. Although, one could understand why a ruler must be ruthless. Considering the times, you would've had to give the citizens something to fear, lest there be a struggle for power through rebellion and treachery. However, many practices were excessively wicked.

One of these particular tyrants was Nabis, ruler of Sparta from 207 BC to 192 BC. Nabis slithered his way into power by murdering two claimants to the Spartan throne. He sustained his rule over the people of Sparta by releasing the prisoners that were held within the land. He assigned these vindictive and ruthless savages to be his own mercenary policing force. Further, Nabis regularly dragged in wealthy landowners to be shaken down for gold and riches. To make this process easier, Nabis created a terrifying instrument of persuasion. Named and fashioned after his wife, the Apega was a female statue that was fitted with spring-released spikes within its hollow interior. The victim was placed inside the arms of the device after they were sprung open. It didn't take much convincing after the spikes began to pierce. If the nobleman was not killed during this encounter, he may have been exiled from his lands. Although it is not known what this device actually looked like, it was likely the inspiration for another instrument of torture, the iron maiden. Nabis was eventually betrayed and assassinated by an Aetolian commander who came to his aide after a defeat in battle. Cavalry commander Alexamenus unexpectedly rushed and speared Nabis to death with a lance as he approached the brigade. This marked the end of an independent Sparta forever. They soon joined the Achaean League, and would never again regain their place as a powerful sovereign state in Greece.

The early Romans also had some sadistic emperors throughout their time. The Caesars, in particular, had been expected to invent novel forms of punishment. They were notorious for inventing new offenses in order to exercise these novel torments. The second Roman emperor, Tiberius Caesar, was certainly an enigmatic oddball who set the standard for future generations. He was said to have been incredibly paranoid and intolerant, and condemned people on a daily basis for the most trivial of circumstances. At the time of his reign, it was illegal to sentence virgin females to death. However, Tiberius found a loophole by having the executioner rape them before putting them to death. Try to imagine living in a society where a teenage girl may be lawfully penalized with rape and strangulation for committing a minor act of transgression. In the work *The Lives of the Twelve Caesars*, by contemporaneous ancient Roman historian Suetonius, translated to English, it was written:

"It is a long story to run through his acts of cruelty in detail; it will be enough to mention the forms which they took, as samples of his barbarity. Not a day passed without an execution, not even those that were sacred and holy; for he put some to death even on New Year's Day. Many were accused and condemned with their children and even by their children."

One story in particular that Suetonius described tops the charts as the most unprovoked yet mildly amusing tortures to date. While Tiberius was visiting the island of Capri, an enthusiastic angler attempted to offer him up a large fish that he had recently caught. However, the man approached the emperor from the rear and startled him. For only this reason, Tiberius had the man's face rubbed with the fish's scales until his skin tore off. After the fisherman received his punishment, he candidly thanked his lucky stars that he hadn't given him the large crab that he also caught. Upon hearing this, Tiberius ordered his men to fetch the crab and instructed them to rip the man's face apart with it, as well.

Thinking about how this whole scenario must have transpired, I imagine Tiberius as a pissed off Joe Pesci. "You wanna give me a fish?" He points at the fisherman, "You wanna give me a fish, eh?" "I'll give you a fuckin' fish." He turns to his guards, "Eh, rub that fuckin' fish on this guy's face until his fuckin' skin falls off."

Ravages of Religion

In 381 AD, Roman emperor Theodosius II attempted to unify the empire with a papal disciplinary council to enforce and resolve matters of faith and punishment. With that, the First Council of Constantinople was established. The council wasted no time. In their first of seven canons, with their dogmatic condemnation of apostates, they legalized the banishment and execution of heretics. To clarify, excommunication and banishment was the common punishment for heresy. Contrary to popular belief, although death by fire was the preferred method of execution for heretics, it was extremely rare for such a punishment to occur. Even so, when the heretic was executed, it was usually the result of secular court decisions. The inquisition was initially meant to save souls who had gone astray. Theodosius and the council decreed:

> "let not these and the Manicheans, who are arisen to the height of impiety, have the liberty of dwelling anywhere within the dominions of the Roman Empire: let the Manicheans be expelled from every city, and punished with death; for they are not to be suffered to have

any dwelling on the earth, lest they should
infect the very elements themselves."

Subsequently, the universal religious persecution of
renouncers was nothing more than commonplace, practiced
traditionally for hundreds of years. Wide-reaching populations
were held hostage by a totalitarian Catholic entity capable of
condemning them for arbitrary thought crimes. With so many
people being banished and excommunicated from society,
there began a revolt. Consequently, dissenters threatened war
against Catholicism. This threat triggered immediate action
from ecclesiastical leaders, whom ordered stricter
punishments for convictions of heresy. This lead to the
founding of the Holy Inquisition by Pope Innocent III. It was
formally established in 1229 in a southern French province
then called Languedoc. In 1242, two Catholic monks were
slaughtered and mutilated by a dozen axe wielding Cathars.
The Cathars were a sect of Christianity that believed the Old
Testament God was Satan. This prompted the Albigensian
Crusade, which nearly eradicated the Cathar stronghold in
Montségur, located in the heart of Languedoc. It was there
that the sanctuary of Cathars was decimated and the
survivors were questioned about their faith. All those who
were captured and refused to denounce their crimes of heresy
against the Catholic faith were burned to death. Around 210

members of the Cathar church willingly marched right into a giant pyre, resembling the unholy pit of Hell on Earth. Fearing that some Cathars escaped, the impractical decision to kill everyone and let God recognize his own led to the legitimacy of using holy inquisitors.

Although the Holy Inquisition was meant to intimidate and resolve heresy, it initially did not implement torture as common practice. In this regard, it appears the Inquisition was much more lenient than secular courts. However, in the year 1252, Pope Innocent IV promulgated the papal bull 'Ad exstirpanda,' which permitted the use of torture to elicit confessions from suspected heretics. The inquisitors were required to obey and enforce this public decree by threat of excommunication. The bull limited torture to not cause loss of limb or life, to be used only once, and to be used only in cases where the suspect was obviously guilty after many proofs. Although this is true as it is written, there are loopholes that were used to get around most of it. For instance, since the person in question could only be tortured once, inquisitors considered the time between each torture as "interruptions" and could have the torture "renewed" at any time. For this reason, most confessions were not retracted after the torture was halted.

Many years later, with the last of the three inquisitions, truly evil cruelties of man became institutionalized. The Spanish Inquisition, established in 1478 by Queen Isabella and King Ferdinand II, is when we would see merciless bone-breaking tortures systematically implemented by the papal court.

To present the topic fairly, there are many who argue on the side of the church. You see, at this time in history, not only was the church a religious institution, but it was also the very fabric by which societies were held together. The Catholic Church punitively maintained principles and ethical standards to ensure the continuation of society. It was responsible for government, education, and the law. Because of this, they profoundly believed that heretics were an essential threat to the sustainability of civilization. This is why they dealt with them so mercilessly. Further, during the times of the Inquisition, torture until death was not meant to punish the condemned. The Inquisition was a purifying counsel meant to save astray souls from evil. They thought that the pain endured prior to death cleansed the soul and exercised them from demons. After death, their belief was that the infected soul would go to purgatory for further tortures until being fully purified. Only then would the tortured soul ascend to Heaven.

On the other hand, there were many instances when amateur executioners attempted to ease the suffering of their victims. When the devout Catholic, Queen Mary I, otherwise known as "Bloody Mary," took to the English throne in 1553, she vowed to eradicate Protestantism. Convinced that Protestants were the source of all evil, she burned some 300 people at the stake, including many bishops and religious leaders. When Bishop Hooper was sent to the stake, it was a merciful gesture to wrap two bags of gunpowder around his neck to swiftly dispatch of him. However, something went terribly wrong. The incompetent executioner was using green wood, which burns incredibly slow. While his lower extremities incinerated at a horrifying pace, the only thing he could do was beg for more fire. Imagine that: experiencing a reality which makes you beg to be engulfed by flames. The sorry executioner frantically stacked more green wood, but with little effect. If that wasn't enough, once the fire did reach the bags of gunpowder, they failed to explode. Whereas it usually took only about 15 minutes, Bishop Hooper took nearly 45 minutes to succumb to the fire. Some said that towards the end, with the swelling of his tongue, he could no longer scream coherently, so he resorted to pounding on his chest. He was so persistent that even after an arm fell off, he kept hammering away with the other until finally surrendering to the flames.

Ironically, Mary's successor, Queen Elizabeth I, detested Catholics. Completely flipping the law, she believed it was her divine mission to turn England into a Protestant country. During her reign, which started in 1558, only five years after Queen Mary had initiated her Protestant genocide, Queen Elizabeth had 123 Catholic priests hanged, drawn and quartered, and many others tortured in various ways. Many were tormented on the rack, which was a platform with straps and pulleys meant to stretch the person until their joints dislocated. With such a drastic shift in the paradigm of state-accepted religion, one could only dream of the fear that the public lived with on a day-to-day basis.

Torture on Demand

There is certainly something to be said about the pleasure that is derived from witnessing acts of cruelty. Although it may be easy to simply call it "sadism", the actual explanation may be much more complicated than that. From the book *Psychopathia Sexualis* (1884), written by the renowned psychiatrist Richard Krafft-Ebing, he offers two examples of "sadistically constituted persons." In both cases, the men received gratuitous sexual gratification from watching the torture, mutilation, and death of animals. He explains that although acts of cruelty to any living entity may provide sexual gratification, it would be silly to link the pleasure from viewing all acts of cruelty with sadism. However, he does say that although a small subconscious connection to sadism may often be present, it is not necessarily the primary incentive.

Krafft-Ebing explains that cruelty is natural to primitive man. Compassion, being a secondary impulse, comes much later in our responses. The concept of "the criminal" was engendered within us through the development of societies, and it triggers "the enemy" instinct within us. It is the natural instinct within all of us to fight, conquer, and destroy. My question is: what does it actually mean to be civilized? Is endorsing and celebrating the torture and execution of a condemned man uncivilized? If it is, then that would mean we have not ever been civilized. If this is the case, then we should change the definition of the word. Instead, what if that is the very thing that makes us civilized? Krafft-Ebing writes:

> "The instinct to fight and destroy, so important an endowment in prehistoric conditions, is long afterward operative; and, in the ideas engendered by civilization, like that of "the criminal," it finds new objects, even though its original object—"the enemy"—still exists. That not simply the death, but also torture, of

the conquered is demanded, is in part explained by the sense of power, which satisfies itself in this way; and in part by the insatiableness of the impulse of vengeance."

When an enemy is captured, it is in our nature to not only kill, but to torture and gratify our insatiable compulsion for vengeance as a collective. Although the criminal has not directly harmed the common medieval onlooker, the intense emotion and rage exhumed from their loins tells a story of personal betrayal. A marvel of humanity.

In my view, these public acts of cruelty are a kind of pre-death celebration ritual. "We captured the enemy; now let's show him what we're capable of!" This could be no different from the posthumous celebration of putting the head of your slain foe on a spear and parading it around town. Humor me and imagine if the human head could survive for days after amputation. In that case, we know that people would have played with recently decapitated heads much more than they already have. We know this because the torture and humiliation element would make it a much more attractive activity. In the same way, intense and impressionable sights of torment are what attracted people to public executions. The torture and execution of condemned prisoners offered the spectator opportunities to fulfill their natural desires for vengeance, power, and influence. This was a delicacy, considering that the feeble plebeians would otherwise never obtain these sentiments.

Common in the 1700s, the pillory was a judicial proxy torture device meant to use public indignation as punishment. The pillory was a simple wooden slab with holes cut out of it attached to a standing pole. The prisoner's neck and wrists were latched inside the holes and he was forced to stand there for typically one hour while a sign attached to him described his crimes. This punishment attracted huge mobs, and depending on the severity of the offenses, the prisoner frequently ended up with serious injuries. For this punishment, the harshness of the crimes reflected the reaction of the mob. For the indolent bystander, it was an entertaining show to be beholding. If a man was sent to the pillory for a small civil infraction, he might have been humiliated and pelted with feces and rotten vegetables. However, these attacks with dung and decaying plant matter still did have the potential to be fatal. Since the person could not guard their face, many times their head was buried in so much feces and urine that they would suffocate to death.

In 1732, John Waller, a notorious con artist and convicted robber, was murdered by an angry mob while on the pillory for a mere 8 minutes. The crowd was shouting obscenities while pelting him with rotten eggs and animal carcasses. They eventually pulled the pillory down and stomped him so hard they cracked his skull and broke his ribs. He died right there on the platform.

Punishment by Confinement

Regarding the most "civilized" society in the world, if you were to assume that the number of offenses punishable by death would decrease as the early-modern era approached, you would be wrong. In England, from the 17th to the late 18th century, the number of crimes punishable by death dramatically increased from 50 to 220. This was highly controversial, and citizens were worried that these new laws were being set in place as a form of class war promulgated by aristocrats. Because of this, lawmakers sought to invent other means of punishment in order to both deter future offenders and restore faith in justice with the masses. This led to the birth of an organized 'punishment by confinement' prison system, similar to what we see in today's world. Unbeknownst to the common citizen, the conditions of these early prisons were not unlike scenes out of Dante's *Inferno*.

Previously, although dungeons had often been used for imprisonment, they were mainly places for temporary detention. They merely detained the prisoner until they received their punishment. These confinement chambers were spread out in various locations, such as in castles, fortresses, cellars, mills, and towers. These makeshift prisons were essentially contracted to individuals who were willing to house prisoners for profit. However, as you would expect, this business had a ridiculously high amount of liability. Not only would the franchisor be responsible for holding and maintaining a potentially dangerous criminal, but if a prisoner escaped, the jailer faced harsh penalties for negligence. It was not like your typical 'Bed and Breakfast.' The inmate did not get a bed and only ate if they arranged to pay for it somehow. Sick inmates dwelled with the rest of the population, so communal diseases were commonplace. Any long-term sentence in some of these deteriorated dungeons of filth meant certain death.

This is an interesting contrast to modern society, where incarceration is the last resort in reforming a criminal. In medieval Europe, the more widely dispensed punishments were public humiliation, torture, exile, and penal servitude.

Now that we have gone over the psychological, causal, and

punitive aspects of these serial killers' lives, let's dive into our first biopic. And who better than the original killer clown himself...

Chapter 4

John Wayne Gacy "The Killer Clown"

A clown can get away with murder. —
John Wayne Gacy

oderly known as "The Killer Clown", John Wayne Gacy Jr. is one of America's most prolific pedophiliac rapist serial killers ever. He is responsible for the slaying of 33 boys and young men and likely many more that he would not admit to. John was born on the unfortunate day of March 17, 1942 in Chicago, Illinois. His mother was a homemaker and his father was a mechanic, World War I veteran, alcoholic, and asshole. Of course, his father beat him regularly. Like many abused children, Gacy Jr. tried to make his father proud of him, only to continuously fail with devastating emotional consequences.

By the age of four, Gacy's father was relentlessly beating him with a leather belt. If you're trying to raise a serial killer, this is completely reasonable punishment for a toddler who spilt milk on the floor. His father once knocked John unconscious with a broomstick and regularly belittled him in front of his sisters. He often called him "dumb" or "stupid" and frequently told him that he would "grow up to be queer." Based on my own elementary studies (learned from the second grade), I believe his father was a miserable, emotionally damaged man, and the only way he could cope with his own failures and feelings of insignificance was to physically and mentally abuse an innocent person. Sounds familiar, doesn't it? Ultimately, the true victims of John Jr.'s cruel upbringing were those whom he manipulated and murdered later in life.

Johns' sexual perversions outwardly manifested at the early age of seven. In 1949, he was busted for fondling a girl at school. When his father found out about this, he very reasonably beat and whipped John with a razor strop. Again, a sensible way to deal with a troubled youth... Ironically, the same year that he sexually assaulted that little girl, a "family friend" who conveniently took him out for car rides molested John. I believe this could have been an early awakening of his homosexual tendencies, as is typically seen in boys who become sexually subjugated by older men. This warrants the term "getting turned out." I think this is the case because Gacy often said that he hated homosexuals and that he was "probably" bisexual, as if admitting to being gay would be damaging to his reputation. It seems like he was confused and detached and didn't know how to sexually identify. Even more, it appears that his homosexual life was shrouded in hatred, secrecy, and thrill, while his heterosexual sex life was plain, ordinary, and monotonous. As far as we know, not once did he tie up any women to sexually torture them to death with a giant dildo. He did, however, have many romantic and successful relationships with women. With that, I think we could agree that his sexual deviances were highly perverted. Regardless, sexuality is extremely complicated, and we could never truly know why he raped and murdered only people of the same sex. Who knows; maybe he was gay and preferred to identify as a bisexual rapist serial killer rather than a gay one.

Throughout his early school years, Gacy was an average student and seemed to lead the life of an ordinary kid. He even had a circle of friends that he was close with. Gacy was also quite the *goody-little-two-shoes* and would often volunteer to aid the truancy officer and run errands for teachers. However, by the fourth grade, he began to suffer blackouts as a result of the relentless beatings incurred on him by his father. He often required hospitalization after suffering from these spells.

His father thought John was faking this to gain sympathy and would be there to bring him down. His father may have been correct. Nonetheless, during this period of Johns' life, his father did regularly beat him without provocation. He used

Gacy's torso as a living punching bag like he was training for the World's Heavyweight Boxing Championship. After all of this, Gacy did not espouse hatred for his father, later claiming to have never fought back.

When Gacy turned 18, he became involved in politics, even becoming a Democratic Party candidate. However, his father, who was still a large part of Gacy Jr.'s life, accused him of pathetically trying to gain acceptance, frequently calling him a "patsy" for being a Democrat. His father would be there to find a way, somehow, to ridicule John, constantly trying to kill his confidence and make him feel useless.

Gacy finally had enough of it, and in his senior year he dropped out of school and ran off to Las Vegas where he was soon employed as a mortuary attendant (he was a janitor). This was where Gacy had his first brush with necrophilia. How romantic... Do you think he brought flowers with him? Lit a few candles? Positioned them with love atop the autopsy table? You know, for that passionate moment when the ambiance needs to be just right. John Wayne Gacy Jr., a Casanova.

Seriously, the actual story is twisted. Each night, Gacy waited until late in the afterhours before skulking out of his cot to view the corpses in the embalming room. Eventually, Gacy's perversions got the best of him, and he climbed into the coffin of a dead teenage boy. He began to kiss, caress, embrace, and enjoy him, eventually pulling his pecker out to have sex with the embalmed body.

As disgusting as it sounds, one could only envision how revolting something like this must have looked. Imagine, if you will, an awkward, acne-riddled, chubby 18-year-old John Wayne Gacy rubbing his sloppy body along a casket as he stares at a child's corpse, licking his lips like a hungry jackal. While gawking at the body, he grabs at his groin right before jumping in and molesting the youthful cadaver. Let us agree that it's hard to visualize anything more repulsive than that.

Gacy later stated that in the midst of romanticizing the corpse, a flash of white light shocked his nervous system. He had to stop what he was doing and get the hell out of there. It's as if Gacy experienced a moment of realization, and in coming very close to committing necrophilia, he managed to creep himself out. I would not doubt that he didn't understand why he climbed into that coffin in the first place. Rather, he did not want to face the truth until after his primal sexual impulses were fulfilled. Regardless, he panicked and moved back home to Chicago that same night. At this time in Gacy's life, he would rather be abused by his father than to face the monster that he was becoming, as if Gacy used his father as the constitution by which he was able to remain grounded. At eighteen years old, this was a very confusing time for Gacy.

On paper, things seemed rather normal, and after receiving a business degree, he moved on to become a semi-successful salesman. He later joined his local Jaycee, an organization of young entrepreneurs and business-minded individuals who encourage leadership and the development of their skills. I think he was already a tremendous salesman, considering everyone was sold on thinking he was a normal guy. He even convinced his co-worker turned wife, Marlynn Myers, whom he married in 1964.

The following year, Gacy became vice-president of the Springfield Jaycees, and continued to fool his friends and family into thinking he was a model citizen. Later on, in the 1960s, Gacy moved to Iowa, where he caught his first criminal sexual conduct charge. In 1967, Gacy lured a 15-year-old boy named Mark Miller (the son of a fellow Jaycee member) into his basement with the promise of alcohol and pornography. Gacy was becoming eager for these perverted experiences and he desperately craved sexual attention from young boys, like an addict with heroin. He got Miller drunk and tricked the boy into being tied up, afterwards sodomizing him without consent. Miller went to the police and reported the rape. Four months later, Gacy hired another boy to mace and beat up Mark, but he fought back and was able to escape the attack.

At age 28, Gacy was eventually convicted of the charges of sodomy and was sentenced to ten years in prison, incurring the maximum sentence possible for such a crime. However, only 18 months later, Gacy was released for good behavior. Regardless, the damage was already done to his home life. Marlynn divorced Gacy and disappeared with their son while he was incarcerated.

Gacy was later said to have blackmailed many boys into performing oral sex on him. Also, he often fooled teenagers into giving him sexual favors by calling them "scientific experiments" and "studies". Each kid was paid up to $50 for the favor. It's amazing how easy it was for him to get away with something so brazen and how seemingly effortless it was for him to get kids to do these things. Who in their right mind would do this? Acknowledging that this actually happened, one can only hope that this was contingent on the fact that we were dealing with goddamned John Wayne Gacy.

The most troubling part about the history of John Wayne

Gacy (for me) to discover was the sadistic creation of his "Pogo" persona. At age 33, Gacy joined the Jolly Joker Clown Club, where he took on the character "Pogo the Clown." He performed at fundraising events, children's hospitals, and even kids' birthday parties. This is the epitome of a pedophiliac predator; someone who puts themselves in the position of being around children with the intent of harming and assaulting them. Looking at his choice of makeup (designed by Gacy himself), it appears he intentionally made Pogo to appear as the classic killer clown. With sharp, jagged edges drawn about his face, he appeared to intentionally give off an exaggeratedly wicked grin, whereas the traditional clown makeup is rounded, appearing more appealing and friendly. As I look at various photos of him, I frequently notice that Gacy seems to have a permanent maniacal look on his face, even without the makeup. It's as if an overflow of sadistic thoughts perpetually oozed out of his thick cranium, forcing him to display an evil expression.

If he was not creepy enough, Gacy was also known to regularly visit his favorite local bar wearing the full evil clown regalia. Personally, I prefer to wear a pair of sweatpants and a tee shirt on my laundry days.

During his Pogo era, Gacy was in a full-blown murder

frenzy. He raped and killed dozens of people until finally confessing to massacring at least 25-33 young men and boys between the years of 1972-1978. Most of them he lured to his house alone, although he did say that he often committed "doubles," killing two boys in one night. He claimed that most of them were young teenage run-aways and male prostitutes that he conveniently abducted from the bus station after nightfall, although this was not completely true.

Gacy also revealed that he had been inspired by the device used in the Houston mass murders, which was a two-by-four fitted with handcuffs. Gacy's murders usually took place between the hours of 3 and 6 AM, and once dead, he hid the cadavers underneath his bed as he slept. He kept them there sometimes for up to 24 hours, depending on what else was going on in the house.

Most of the bodies were hidden within the crawlspace in his home. It was there that, after murdering his victims, Gacy dug shallow graves and poured quicklime over the bodies to speed up the decomposition process. He also admitted to embalming some of the bodies in his garage before burial, which he no doubt learned from his time as a mortuary attendant. Ole Gacy boy was a bit of a jack of all graves.

Gacy murdered his first victim, 15-year-old Timothy McCoy, in January of 1972. Believe it or not, this murder was a total fluke. It was a perfectly reasonable accident. Gacy met Timothy at a Chicago Greyhound bus terminal and enticed him to his home for a free place to spend the night. In the morning, Gacy woke to find McCoy standing in his bedroom with a knife. Without hesitation, Gacy lunged toward the boy and snatched the knife out of his hand. Before muttering a single word, Gacy frantically stabbed at the boy, viciously killing him right then and there.

After inspecting his house, Gacy found that McCoy was merely preparing breakfast and had been inviting Gacy to eat with him. Instead of calling the police and reporting the incident, Gacy did what any normal person would do: he buried McCoy in a shallow grave in the crawlspace under his home. In his later confession, Gacy stated that he ejaculated while murdering McCoy, saying, "That's when I realized that death was the ultimate thrill."

Gacy's second victim (who remains unidentified) was a bit of a crash course for John. After strangling him to death, he learned that he had to stuff clothes into his victims' mouths, because fluid eventually expelled from their orifices, and carelessly shoveling them into his closet wasn't sanitary enough.

Around July of 1975, Gacy targeted an employee of his own contracting business. It was 16-year-old roofer, John Butkovich, whom disappeared after relentlessly hounding Gacy for back-pay owed. Butkovich's body was the first of two found on day one of the digging underneath Gacy's garage and crawlspace. Although Gacy eventually confessed to these murders, there is no documented account of how he killed Butkovich. However, Gacy did explain that he became efficient at binding his victims through a "trick" that he showed them.

Gacy handcuffed himself behind the back, and with a key in his rear pocket, he let himself free, with how he did it unbeknownst to the second party. After removing the handcuffs, he would give them an opportunity to try. I have to admit that this is a rather clever way to convince someone to willingly be handcuffed. Once shackled, after a bit of a struggle, Gacy reveals his ploy, "The trick is you have to have the key." Gacy is now in full control of his victim.

After confessing to the murders, Gacy explained how the assault and murder would happen once the victims were immobilized. Gacy usually muffled their screams with their own underwear and commenced choking them from behind with a rope attached to a two-by-four as he sodomized them. This is most likely what happened to Butkovich.

When Butkovich went missing, his parents reportedly called the police over a hundred times, urging them to investigate Gacy further. It seems that catching petty drug dealers was a much more important task than investigating the sudden disappearance of teens. Gacy was able to continue with his onslaught for nearly 3 more years. Let us take a moment and stand up to give the Des Plaines Police Department a blank expression and slow clap for their hard work.

After murdering an unconfirmed number of young men and boys, Gacy actually showed "mercy" to one. On December 30th, 1977, Gacy abducted 19-year-old Robert Donnelly at gunpoint. He took him to his home where he began torturing and sodomizing him with various objects. After having his head dunked repeatedly in the bathtub, Robert was in such agony that he asked Gacy to kill him, to which Gacy replied, "I'm getting 'round to it." After many more hours of torturing Robert – for whatever reason – Gacy loaded him into his car, drove him to his place of work, and released him.

When Robert reported this to the police, Gacy told them

that he had a love-slave relationship with the man, and that the entire thing was consensual. The police believed Gacy, and there was no further investigation. The incompetence level of the police in some of these cases is absolutely astounding.

Gacy's Capture and Execution

The end of his murder career began with the disappearance of a 15-year-old boy named Robert Piest. Gacy met him at a local pharmacy while he was giving an estimate for construction work to be done on the building. While Piest was shopping, he overheard Gacy saying that he regularly hired teenage boys to work for him. Piest struck up a conversation with Gacy about a possible job opportunity. Gacy obliged and offered to take him along for a ride. Robert mentioned this to his mother, telling her that he was going off with a contractor who offered him work. After leaving with Gacy in his truck, Piest was never heard from again.

Upon the initiation of the investigation, police immediately noticed a reoccurring connection with Gacy and the disappearance of boys. They finally decided to take it seriously when they looked up Gacy's history and found that he was previously convicted of sodomy with a minor.

Detectives questioned the pharmacy owner who had previously talked with Gacy about the estimate. He named "John Gacy" as the man who likely offered Robert the job.

Subsequently, after constantly being surveilled and followed by investigators, it began to wear on Gacy. The police continued to gather more evidence which suggested that Gacy murdered Piest. They found suspicious items, such as a gun, handcuffs, a boy's class ring, and the two-by-four with holes drilled in it. This was easily obtained from his home with their first search warrant. However, they failed to discover any bodies at that time and had to let Gacy go free after a brief initial interrogation.

Gacy eventually broke and gave a lengthy verbal confession to his lawyer after being relentlessly shadowed by police. Immediately, a second search warrant was issued, and investigators noticed the smell of rotting corpses coming from a heating duct in his bathroom. Soon, they began to dig, and Gacy began to sing.

As soon as he was told that they were excavating his home, Gacy said that he wanted to "Clear the air." He commenced his confession to murdering around 30 people ranging from the ages of 14 to 21.

Consequently, Gacy was charged with 33 murders in 1980, and was said to be a "paranoid schizophrenic suffering from multiple personality disorder" by three psychiatrists. He was also previously diagnosed with an antisocial personality back in 1968 due to his ability to commit rape without showing any signs of remorse. After being sentenced, he was sent to Menard Correctional Center to be on death row for a grueling 14 years.

While incarcerated, he was stabbed in the arm with a shank by the infamous I-57 killer Henry Brisbon. Unfortunately, Gacy didn't incur any serious injuries. Henry should have aimed for his dick.

His last meal consisted of shrimp, a bucket of KFC chicken, french fries, and an entire pound of strawberries. Finally, after the public eagerly waited 14 years, in 1994, Gacy was executed by method of a semi-botched lethal injection. It took him a total of eighteen minutes to die after one of the IVs clogged up. Typically, death occurs within the first seven minutes of injection. Lethal injection is actually quite a mild form of execution. It may be the most civilized form of capital punishment developed to date. Basically, it consists of three different intravenous injections. The first solution is meant to render the subject unconscious, the second to induce muscle paralysis, and the third to cause cardiac arrest. Gacy got it good, folks. He essentially died in his sleep. His last words were reportedly directed toward an officer, to whom he said, "Kiss my ass."

John Wayne Gacy's Medieval Punishment

Now for the fun part! I will act as the engineer of his execution had he been convicted of these crimes in medieval times. My choice of execution takes in to account the methods of murder and torture that Gacy inflicted upon his victims. I choose impalement.

A little background... Impaling is one of the most brutal forms of torture and execution ever derived by man. In the Ottoman Empire, the impaled were closely watched and carefully impaled by artisans or *masters*. These masters impaled the condemned directly through the anus with a large, wide wooden rod. They propped them up high in the air, yet ensured that the stake missed every internal organ, to guarantee the sufferer not die from organ failure or blood loss. They stayed atop the wooden rod so long that they died from either dehydration or starvation. The longer the condemned remained alive atop the pole, the more earnings the master was allotted for their duties. The longer the torture, the more they were paid. Those Ottomans were not screwing around.

From various sources, we know that these wooden rods weren't particularly sharp. Once the person was lifted into the air, it could take days for them to gradually slide down the pole. It eventually exits through the mouth, chest, or shoulder. A truly gifted master impaler makes sure the pole exits through the mouth or throat. From the written account of a Genoese merchant within the Ottoman Empire by the name of Jacopo dei Campi, we have a description of Turkish impalement:

"Diverse and horrible are the punishments, injustices, and cruelties of the Grand Turk. The most usual death he metes out to anyone he pleases, whether guilty of any crime or not, is to make the man he wishes to punish lie down on the ground; a sharp long pole is placed in the rectum; with a big mallet held in both hands the executioner strikes it with all his might, so that the pole, known as a palo, enters the human body, and according to its path, the unfortunate lingers on or dies at once; then he raises the pole and plants it in the ground; thus the unfortunate is left in extremis"

Another chilling firsthand account is that of 17th century French explorer and scientist Jean de Thévenot, who kept extensive writings of his travels. While traveling through Egypt, regarding Egyptian execution, Jean observed and recorded many punishments:

"They lay the Malefactor upon his Belly, with his Hands tied behind his Back, then they slit up his Fundament with a Razor, and throw into it a handful of Paste that they have in readiness, which immediately stops the Blood. After that they thrust up into his Body a very long Stake as big as a Mans Arm, sharp at the point and tapered, which they grease a little before; when they have driven it in with a Mallet, till it come out at his Breast, or at his Head or Shoulders, they lift him up, and plant this Stake very streight in the Ground, upon which they leave him so exposed for a day. One day I saw a Man upon the Pale, who was Sentenced to continue so for three Hours alive and that he might not die too soon, the Stake was not thrust up far enough to come out at any part of his Body, and they also put a stay or rest upon the Pale, to hinder the weight of his body from making him sink down upon it, or the point of it from piercing him through, which would have presently killed him: In this manner he was left for some Hours, (during which time he spoke) and turning from one side to another, prayed those that passed by to kill him, making a thousand wry Mouths and Faces, because of the pain be suffered when he stirred himself, but after Dinner the Basha sent one to dispatch him; which was easily done, by making the point of the Stake come out at his Breast, and then he was left till next Morning, when he was taken down, because he stunk horridly. Some have lived upon the Pale until the third day, and have in the mean while smoaked Tobacco, when it was given to them."

One cannot mention impalement without discussing the man whom used it as his own sick form of entertainment, coining the nickname *Vlad the Impaler*. He was also the inspiration for the caricature of Count Dracula. Vlad was infamous for impaling thousands of people during his Romanian reign in the 1400s, striking fear amongst his enemies. He even went as far as impaling entire armies while he watched and feasted.

A story of Vlad's ferociousness was once told regarding one of these feasts when Vlad was eating alongside a fellow nobleman. Vlad asked the man if he enjoyed the smell of rotting men while they ate, to which the nobleman replied, "No." So Vlad, being a logical-minded and sane individual, ordered the man to be impaled higher than all others so the smell wouldn't reach him.

Imagine if you were able to fly a hot air balloon over the horrifying panorama when Vlad ordered the impalement of an entire 25,000-man army. For reference, this amount of people is roughly the capacity of your standard American college football stadium. Visualize that many people lined up in a vast area of land with their hands tied. You see thousands of figures cascaded over mountains of giant wooden spears. Then, acres of giant rods spiking out of the ground with thousands of skewered men atop of them, crying out, begging for death as a delighted voivode looks on from his castle's balcony while merrily feasting on turkey legs and wine. Branded into your mind, the sound of the distant, collective screams are enough for you to desperately try to forget it.

With Vlad, impaling could happen in various ways. The

impaled may be skewered through the neck, chest, mouth, or anus, mostly for decoration purposes. Considering that Vlad left the bodies to rot as a way to invoke fear among his enemies, he intentionally created an artificial forest made up entirely of closely scattered tree-like spears with decaying corpses to appear as foliage. From afar, it may have looked as any other forest. As you gradually approached, the horrendous scene and vile odor would have become progressively more evident. This was an effective deterrent to incoming enemy armies. Once they realized what they were seeing, they would drop to their knees and pray for their fallen brethren. Demoralized, they usually turned back.

Personally, I prefer the Ottomans' technique. As the engineer of Gacy's execution, I get to do what I want... Gacy's death would be the slow, methodical impaling from a bankrupt master impaler who gambled away his last coin the night prior.

Gacy's big day commences with a swift kick to the dick upon waking in his muddy cell. He is shackled and marched barefoot over gravel to the impalement grounds. While entering the designated area, Gacy observes an expressionless executioner fashioning a dulled spike out of pine wood. Shackled, Gacy is hastily forced to the ground, after which the spike is swiftly thrust into his anus. Then, with the artisan directing four soldiers, they successfully lift him into the air and secure the bottom of the pole into the ground. Gacy squeals and flails as the pole slowly inches its way through his pelvis and abdomen. The soldiers find Gacy particularly funny, so they sit on the lush grass and taunt him into making barnyard noises. They throw small rocks and spit at him as he cries out for a mercy blow from one of their weapons. The agonizing, slow-moving probe continues as Gacy sways in and out of consciousness. Eventually, the spear exits through his front collar region. Gacy is still alive at this point. Slowly progressing, the rod pierces through the digastric muscle under his jaw and his full body weight is consequently held up only by his skull. With the full weight of his body supported by the stake lodged into the roof of his mouth, Gacy is suddenly unable to beg for a quick death. Wearily opening his eyes, Gacy is paralyzed with pain and exhaustion. The only thing heard is a weak muffled whimper as he gradually approaches death by dehydration. The last thing Gacy experiences before death is the taste of his own shit-stained asshole... This certainly gives a whole new meaning to the phrase *ass to mouth*.

Chapter 5

Alexander Pichushkin "The Chessboard Killer"

For me, life without murder is like a life without food. —Alexander Pichushkin

Currently known as the worst serial killer in the history of Russia, Alexander Pichushkin was convicted of 48 murders, but admittedly killed 61. His aim was to kill one person for each square on the chessboard, but he was caught 3 short of his goal. However, when asked if he would stop after completing the board, he said that he would never have stopped killing.

Born on April 9th, 1974 in Moscow, Russia, Alexander was said to be a normal kid before an accident occurred that changed him for the rest of his life. While playing on a swing-set in his preteens, he accidentally fell off. After falling backward and smashing his head on the ground, while trying to hold on to the swing, he was forcedly thrust forward. He bashed the front of his head on the pavement, irreparably damaging his frontal lobe.

According to professionals, the frontal lobe regulates attention, reward, planning, and motivation (among other things). Moreover, the frontal lobe is responsible for the brain's ability to understand future repercussions for current actions. It is also reported by the National Institute of Health that damage to the frontal lobe can lead to a slightly increased risk of developing schizophrenia and/or inapt emotional response functions.

After this incident, Alexander's mood and attitude clearly changed. He was no longer paying attention in class and would have wild temper tantrums. This forced his mother to remove him from his regular classes and enroll him in a special education program for the mentally deficient. Not only was this incredibly demoralizing for Alexander, but when approached by his previous classmates, he was bullied, beaten, and called a "retard". This infuriated Alexander and further alienated him from society. I suppose that in this context, you could understand why he developed such hatred towards others. Understand, yes, but some things are unforgiveable. Pichushkin is a grotesque imp whose existence is predicated on wallowing in negativity and a motivation for vengeance.

Alexander's grandfather was skeptical. Early on, he noticed that Alexander had great potential after recognizing that although he was very troubled, he was in fact very intelligent. Naturally, his grandfather opted to mentor Alexander.

His grandfather's hobby was playing chess at the local "Bitsa Park," and soon Alexander developed an incredible talent for the game. Even at a young age, Alexander enrolled in tournaments at the park, going on to defeat even the most experienced of opponents. Alexander stayed with his grandfather until he unexpectedly died, leaving Alexander no choice but to move back home with his mother.

The death of his grandfather was a serious blow to Alexander. As a way to cope, he began drinking vodka heavily. Although he drank along with his chess opponents at the park, it was noticeable that it did not affect his game as it did his challengers. Alexander started to envision this as a mechanism for evil.

In 1992, with plans of murder on his mind, Alexander attempted to recruit a classmate friend to aide him in committing a string of murders. However, when his friend declined to help, Alexander threw him down a sewer. This was Alexander's first murder. Nevertheless, he did not begin his killing campaign until many years later. Of this, we can be certain, since Alexander was very proud of his murders. If he killed any more, we would know about it.

In 1999, at the age of 25, Alexander began his murderous campaign that later captivated Russia. He went on to slay an apparent 60 more people, 48 of which were confirmed. He killed them in various ways, many by throwing them into the unforgiving sewer system beneath Moscow. However, his preferred method was bludgeoning with a hammer. For each murder, Alexander placed a numbered sticker on his personal chessboard, starting at one. He was attempting to kill one person for each of the 64 chess squares. The only fortunate thing about his crimes is that now we can confidently answer the trivia question, "How many squares are there on a checkerboard?"

Over the next 7 years, Alexander befriended locals and homeless people from his neighboring area and entice them to drink vodka with him in Bitsa Park. When they were sufficiently drunk, Alexander attacked, repeatedly hitting them over the head with a hammer. He shoved the broken vodka bottle into the gaping wounds of their cranium. I happen to think that in his own mind, this symbolized the crown of the king or queen, or the knob used to pick up and place each chess piece.

Initially, it appears as though his motives were nonexistent. Pissed off at the world, he simply wanted to kill for the sport of it. He makes it evident that he doesn't even know why he wanted to kill, he felt only as if it were something that he had to do. He had to kill like we have to eat. Nevertheless, Alexander stated that it made him feel like God. Therefore, it is reasonable to assume that he did it for the pleasure he received from overpowering someone and being their angel of death. Seeking a consistent motive, I am inclined to offer my armchair psychological opinion.

Considering that Alexander thought of himself as God when committing these murders becomes a rather interesting concept to grapple with after learning that he is an atheist. Therefore, I personally believe that he was referencing himself as the God of the chessboard; interpreting the world as his own game of chess. Consider this. The King is the one whom is to be protected at all costs. Without the king, everyone dies. The Queen is the dominant force that has unrestricted access to the fortress, total authority. The rest are there to be sacrificed for the well-being of the king. What is greater than both authority and the king? God.

I believe that Alexander created a 65th square, and that square was the entire chessboard. During his murderous campaign, according to Alexander, he was God. He was playing his own sick game as each of his victims represented a chess piece that he had to conquer. In the process, he was conquering the entire board, ultimately becoming God. I think this is why he recorded each of the murders on his chessboard. It was a countdown. Further, I propose that after he hit his mark of 64 kills, he would have committed suicide, thus ultimately ascertaining the grandiose victory of checkmating God. With this in mind, one could only guess who the killing of his final victim "the King," would have been. Would it have ended with a single murder of a famous celebrity or politician? Would he go on a mass murder rampage directed at as many people he could kill in one highly populated area? Luckily, the world may never know.

Regardless of my hypothesis, this is merely a suggestion, and there is no telling what Alexander was thinking without him revealing the actual truth to the public, something which I am certain he will not do.

Pichushkin's Capture and Trial

Unfortunately for Alexander, and fortunately for Russia, he was apprehended on June 14th, 2006. He was finally caught after killing one of his coworkers from the supermarket he worked at. She was 36-year-old single mother Marina Moskalyova.

Alexander was forward with Maria, and she was open to it. She very much liked him and was happy to be going out with him. They were becoming closer, and Maria was very hopeful. They finally made plans for a date, and Alexander had only one thing on his mind; it wasn't sex. He took her out on a private picnic in Bitsa Park. Alexander pulled out his hammer and bashed Marina's head in while she was distracted. He carelessly left her body where she fell. Alexander initially had doubts as to whether he should kill her but said that he would always regret it if he didn't. I concede that I have no idea what that means. It makes me wonder if he tried to have feelings other than hate but was unable to materialize them. Within his damaged mind, could feelings of companionship be linked with the act of killing? However, what he could have meant was that he was regretful over the fact that her death was the reason for him being discovered; I think the latter is most plausible.

After finding Marina's body, police discovered a crucial piece of evidence that lead investigators directly to Alexander. In one of her jacket pockets was a metro ticket. While scanning the videos of the subway, the victim's son came forward with another piece of evidence. Marina left a short letter for him in the kitchen after finding that her phone was broken. In the letter, she stated that she was leaving with "Sasha" (short for Alexander). She also left Alexander's phone number in case her son needed to contact her.

The police viewed Marina on the subway video surveillance and lo and behold, there was Alexander holding a suspicious bag, escorting Marina off the train only hours before her death. This was enough evidence for investigators to make an arrest and charge Alexander with the murder of Miss Moskalyova.

After hours of interrogation, Pichushkin finally confessed to the 15 murders that were discovered in Bitsa Park. However, what shocked police was that he admitted to killing many more than that. Considering that Alexander killed for sport and with no consistency as to whether the victim was male or female, police were astonished to discover the true kill-count.

During his trial, Alexander was placed in a glass cage to protect him from the victim's families. This is where he pompously showboated for the world to see. The trial was made into a cinematic event with mobs of cameras and journalists covering this surreal story. They portrayed Alexander as a real life super villain. Throughout the trial, Alexander paced back and forth in the glass cage, showing no remorse as the gruesome details were being discussed. At the times when a crime was addressed, the judge asked Alexander if he killed a particular person, he either gave a nodding gesture or casually said, "Yes, I killed them."

After taking an hour to read the deliberation, Judge Vladimir Usov sentenced Alexander to life in prison. With the first 15 years to be served in solitary confinement. Unfortunately, Pichushkin will not face the death penalty due to the abolishment of Capital Punishment in Russia in 1996. Had it not been eliminated, Alexander would have faced the firing squad. Although not as satisfying as what may have happened in the dark ages, at least the victims would have had equivalent retribution.

Alexander Pichushkin's Medieval Punishment

In light of Alexander's preferred means of murder by smashing his victims head in with a hammer, I choose... The Spanish Inquisition.

Okay, you might be a little confused with that choice.

Although the Spanish Inquisition was not necessarily a death sentence, if facing any Inquisitors, Alexander would be introduced to the many demented torture devices that were used to squeeze confessions out of people.

For a quick recap, although there were three Inquisitions, the Spanish Inquisition began in 1478. It was initiated by King Ferdinand and Queen Isabella. It was a papal court used to condemn non-Catholics of heresy. If the person in question did not confess their blasphemous crimes against God and follow Catholicism, they were tortured and many times executed. This was mostly done to non-Catholic Christians and foreign converts whom were believed to be insincere about their faith.

Much of the torture that occurred at the hands of the Inquisition was meant to get the person to confess. Regardless, to confess was quite futile, and most of the time if they reached the point of torture, nothing the prisoner said would be good enough. The Spanish Inquisition was particularly ruthless in that it was responsible for the torture and execution of thousands of people for the arbitrary crime of heresy. To support this claim, I will reference one otherwise trivial case in which a nun was put to death by means of a garrote. Garrote is an archaic term used to describe the process of using fine strings to pull tightly around the neck as person chokes to death. This is usually done by using a device to wrap the strings around (together with the device becoming the garrote), tightening the threads as it twists.

In the book *History of The Inquisition from Its Establishment in the Twelfth Century to Its Extinction in the Nineteenth* by William Harris Rule, he describes a case in which a Cistercian nun by the name of Doña Maria Miranda was tried and executed in 1558. When Don Alfonzo, the Lorde of the town, attempted to save the nun's life, the Inquisitors said to him that it was "scandalous to display that much anxiety for a single nun when so many had died for lesser faults."

After she was executed by means of the garrote, her body was burnt. Her crime was that, when hearing a person repeat the following passage, *"Being justified by faith, we have peace with God through our Lord Jesus Christ,"* she thought it sounded right, and believed it, but she understood not in what sense she was meant to believe it. For this only she was put to death. I recount this case in particular to give you a grasp of how absurd and unforgiving the Spanish Inquisition actually was.

This brings me back to Alexander. In 2008, during an interview with the Russian tabloid *Tvoi Den*, Alexander was asked about what he thought about religion. Alexander stated that he was baptized when he was 3 months old. Translated to English, Alexander said:

"The baptism took place, but I did not want it. Well, I do not think that someone ... is there. I can also say that I will not either read the Bible or write an autobiography. I have never prayed to God, never will. This is a beautiful fairy tale. For the weak, for those who sacrifice themselves to the State. Men, as they age, increasingly dream that someone is there who is all powerful."

Seeing that I am the engineer of Pichushkin's demise, I get to choose the time, place, and circumstance by which he is caught and executed. By far, the best place for him to be discovered is Valladolid, Spain, in the 1500s. Considering that Alexander was baptized, he would be a prime target for charges of apostasy, reprimanded only by death.

There is another reason why I place Alexander there. Alexander was incredibly proud of his murders. He even told reporters that his goal was to kill more people than anyone in the history of Russia. Concerning this, and understanding the pride that he felt after recording each of his murders on the chessboard, it would be too gratifying for Alexander to convict him of the kill count.

During his trial, Alexander asked to be convicted of murdering 61 people, but he was only sentenced with the 48 that investigators were able to confirm. Alexander was so upset by this that he said he would happily cut his lawyer open like a fish for not allowing the prosecution to raise the kill count. Regarding this, I would rather Alexander be tortured and executed for apostasy at the discretion of the Inquisition, denying him the satisfaction of completing his objective. Consequently, it would revoke him the opportunity to bask in the infamy and recognition that he desperately desired.

The head crusher was famously used during the Spanish Inquisition as well as throughout much of the dark ages. Considering the head crusher was designed in a way that the prisoner couldn't even speak while under its grip, death was likely to occur from the refusal to confess. Seeing that Alexander was quite a hardheaded man (pardon the pun), it is likely that he would not escape the clutches of the Inquisition. The head crusher was typically used in the worst cases, and without a doubt, stubborn Alexander would have met his end from this device. I find this appropriate for Alexander, taking into consideration his preferred method of murder by bludgeoning.

The head crusher is a horrifying device that was no doubt created by a bastard of a person. It consists of a crown (or cap) attached to a giant screw that – when twisted – slowly crushed the captive's head as their jaw lay flat on a horizontal rail. The screw acts like a vice, and the interrogator slowly smashed the prisoner's head little by little, often taking hours until they were satisfied.

Death often occurred after the prisoner was persistently defiant, refusing to confess. The tormenter commenced turning of the giant screw until the person undoubtedly experienced one of the most painful deaths possible. There is no blocking the pain out of your head with this one...

Observing from our golden throne of justice, we can see it unfold.

Alexander is manhandled and strapped to the device in a dark dungeon. At the first couple turns of the screw, Alexander's jaw is effortlessly broken. The pressure is unrelenting as the screw is wrenched some more. Next, his teeth implode into the skull, each tooth shattering like glass, leaving shards of broken bone as they burst and splinter into his maxilla and lower jaw. The pressure of the vice lingers as the slow twisting continues. At last, the upper portion of his cranium is put under so much pressure that Alexander's eyeballs pop and splatter out of their sockets.

From various sources, it has been said that there are some variations of this device that were equipped with a tray for catching the eyeballs, but I have been unsuccessful in finding any such device to support this claim. Maybe that's the luxury model.

Looking at numerous pictures of Alexander, the one thing that strikes me is how large his forehead is (that thing is more like a sevenhead). Considering the swelling brain damage he incurred when he was young, this was likely incurred then. It would be interesting indeed to see how long his huge noggin could hold up against the head crusher.

Moreover, the fact that the head crusher's crown tended to have a downward-pointed jagged metal brim, it is possible that the pointy bits would have stuck into Alexander's scalp as it was being fastened. This is because the size of the cap was not adjustable, and from what I have seen, the crown does not appear to be very wide. At the very least, this would increase the amount of discomfort he experienced. I imagine the jagged brim would completely tear through his scalp as the mechanism was hardly even wrenched from the start.

Chapter 6

Ted Bundy "The Campus Killer"

I'm as cold a motherfucker as you've ever put your fucking eyes on. I don't give a shit about those people. —Ted Bundy

B orn Theodore Robert Coswell in 1946, Ted Bundy is one of Americas' most well-known serial killers and necrophiles. He has confessed to 30 murders, but over 100 are believed to have transpired. Bundy was a powder keg waiting to go "boom" right from the get-go.

Ted was born at the Elizabeth Lund Home for Unwed Mothers in Burlington, Vermont to a woman named Elanor Louise Crowell. The true name of his father remains a mystery. It has been thought that Ted's own Grandfather, Samuel, could have also been his father, but there is no proof to support this. However, his grandfather and mother raised him together as their own son to avoid the social stigma of raising a bastard child. Eventually, Ted found out for himself that he was in fact born out of wedlock and shunned his mother for it. Rightly so, as his morality was clearly superior to hers. Concerning this, I wonder if Ted actually justified his actions in some weird way.

Like, murdering and raping the cadavers of young women is okay because you can't get a corpse pregnant! It makes sense in a totally non-hypocritical way.

One thing to note: Ted's grandfather was an absolute nutcase. He was a well-known bully who beat his wife and the family dog. It was even said that he swung stray cats by their tails "for fun." He could also be seen arguing and cursing at people who weren't even there, and he was known to have gone into full-blown fits of rage for no apparent reason. Suitably, he was a deacon at his church. Ted's grandmother was described as being an obedient, timid woman who often underwent shock treatment for her depression. If that isn't Americana at its finest, I don't know what is. It's a mystery how Bundy could have possibly grown up to be a serial killer.

Ted's odd behavior began at a very early age. Bundy's aunt awoke from a nap only to find herself surrounded by knives and a three-year-old Ted standing next to her, smiling. Later on, as a kid in the 1950s, Ted could be found in the streets digging through trash cans for old comics and girly magazines. He routinely got drunk and spied on women through their windows as they undressed. Who knows, if the internet existed during this time, Bundy may have just stayed home. In a parallel universe where Bundy is born in a future timeline, murder is averted by internet porn!

Ted did not have a prolific social life, and he usually spent most of his time alone. He admits in interviews that he did not have many social skills and never understood interpersonal relationships. He did eventually fall in love briefly, while attending University of Washington, in 1967. He was also a juvenile delinquent and was arrested in high school numerous times for theft. The things said about Ted so far let us know right away that there was something up with him – possibly a number of things – the most obvious being that he mixed his perversions with his public life.

His first murders are another mystery. It has been said that he attempted his first kidnapping back in 1969, but never murdered anyone until the early 70s. However, in other interviews, he admits to killing two young women while vacationing with his family in the same year as his first attempted kidnapping. It is also believed that as far back as 1961 at the age of 14, he could possibly have been responsible for the kidnapping and murder of an eight-year-old girl, although there is no "hard" evidence, just "circumstantial." Bundy's stories tend to bounce around, and he had a bad habit of contradicting himself. There were also many things he wouldn't admit to at all. One thing is for sure: he sprang into action in the early 70s.

Ted Bundy was a unique kind of serial killer in that he not only stalked, tortured, and killed his victims, but he also had sex with their dead bodies. He would do this until the body was so decomposed that he was physically unable to perform any further sexual acts on it. He also decapitated at least twelve women and took some of their heads home with him to keep as souvenirs. Not so normal these days, but head hunting was commonplace in the dark ages. Bundy was born a few thousand years too late.

Back in 1974, Bundy broke into 18-year-old Joni Lenz' basement in the middle of the night. He broke a metal rod from her own bed frame and proceeded to beat her with it until she was unconscious. Then he raped her badly beaten body with a speculum. Although a horrible event, she did manage to survive this awful attack, but unfortunately she came out of it with permanent brain damage.

About a year later, the body of Lynda Healy was found. Bundy had also broken into her basement while she was sleeping. He beat her and stripped her naked. He dressed her in blue jeans, a white blouse, and boots, and kidnapped her. Eventually, Bundy ended up killing and raping her (in that order). These two brazen murders were the beginning of something truly horrifying. It's people like Bundy who are the reason we extract lead from the Earth to make bullets.

Bundy became addicted to surprise attacks and consequently more and more college girls began disappearing. He began using simple tactics to lure young unsuspecting women into his car. One of his favorites was to pretend to be a disabled man trying to carry heavy items. After enticing them into offering help, Bundy would knock them unconscious as they bent over to put his groceries into his Volkswagen Beetle.

Bundy also pretended to be a police officer, luring women into his car for various "offences." He once revealed that he had told them that he needed them to file a report against someone who damaged their vehicle in the area. Bundy, being a handsome fellow, was able to do this quite frequently. It was seemingly easy for Bundy to charm many of these women into going along with his story. If he resembled someone like Carrot Top, he would not have pulled it off as often as he did.

The masses became very alert after reports of his terrible crimes hit national media. Although the police were fervently working day and night, they had no concrete suspects. They did, however, receive numerous reports of a strange man with his arm in a sling driving a tan/brown Volkswagen Beetle, which later became one of Ted's trademarks.

With the media attention focused on his murders, Ted kept to his studies and in 1974 was accepted into The University of Utah to study law. However, he was very disappointed in the classes, saying that he found them to be "incomprehensible" and that he envied the rest of his classmates for having an intellectual capacity greater than his. Many average people can relate, as this explanation could be used in many areas of life tainted by loss and failure. However, excuses are just that: excuses. I take no pity on Bundy. There is a special place in Hell for Bundy. It's in the ass rape chamber furnished with rusty nail-studded carpet and lemon juice sprinklers.

Ted's murderous rampage finally came to an end when he was stopped by the police in August of 1975. When his car was searched, they found numerous suspicious items, including handcuffs, a crowbar, rope, and a ski mask (which could be linked with other murders). Police thought they were burglary tools, and when questioned, Bundy gave a cock-and-bull story for why he was in possession of such items. His apartment was then searched, and a brochure for ski resorts was indeed found with a check next to The Wildwood Inn, the same resort that one of his victims, Caryn Campbell, was reported missing.

He was then brought in for a line-up and was subsequently identified as "Officer Roseland." Roseland was one of the characters that he made up to fool potential victims, one of whom had escaped from his vehicle when her suspicions superseded his manipulation. He was also identified as the mysterious man who had been lurking around the night when Debbie Kent went missing.

Ted would not go easily though, and during and after his trials he escaped numerous times. His first escape was in 1977, from the Pitkin County Courthouse. He was awaiting trial for the murder of Caryn Campbell, and he asked if he could go to the library. He was given permission, and once the coast was clear he leaped from the second story of the building. With a sprained ankle, he ran to the next town. He even managed to make it up into the mountains and rested for two days in an abandoned cabin. Bundy then stole a Cadillac and nearly made it, but he was caught by two deputies who pulled him over for weaving in and out of traffic. He had been on the run for six days.

He again successfully escaped after being back in custody by somehow managing to get his hands on a hacksaw blade and $500 cash. He sawed through the welds of a small metal plate in the ceiling of his cell. He even took the time to force himself to lose enough weight to eventually fit through the narrow passage. On the night of his great escape, he dressed warmly and stuffed books and paper under his blanket to make it seem like he was asleep. He slipped through the crawl space, and in a matter of time, he was once again free, but now he was caught in the middle of a snowstorm. A Good Samaritan gave Bundy a ride, and he was soon on a flight to Chicago. Prison guards didn't even realize he was missing until 17 hours later, by which time Bundy was already in the windy city.

Once in the city, he caught a train to Ann Arbor, Michigan and got a room at the YMCA. He enjoyed his freedom and even went to a bar to watch the Rose Bowl. Now, I don't know what it is about Michigan that attracts serial killers, but if you notice, many of these serial killers I mention will visit Michigan at one time or another, for whatever reason. Strikes me as a little bit odd, is all.

He went on to steal a car in Michigan and drove it to Atlanta, Georgia, then caught a bus to Florida. Once in Florida, he snagged a room at a boardinghouse and went by the name "Chris Hagen." He often committed petty crimes like purse snatching, shoplifting, and other minor offenses in order to survive while on the run.

However, it didn't take long for his murderous tendencies to get the best of him, and in the wee hours of Super Bowl Sunday morning, he went on to perform one of his most sadistic and notorious attacks of all. He stormed into a sorority house at Florida State University and beat two sleeping women senseless. He went on to beat two other women to death in other rooms throughout the sorority house. He did this in less than half an hour, and after leaving the sorority, he broke into a house not too far away and beat another woman to death.

After accomplishing this, he hit the road again and kidnapped 12-year-old Kimberly Diane Leach from her Junior High School to rape and murder along the way. He dumped her body in a pig shed and continued to travel across the Florida panhandle. If this act alone doesn't seal his fate for the ghastliest medieval punishment imaginable, I don't know what does.

Bundy's Capture and Execution

Police finally caught him again when they pulled him over and ran the license plate number, finding out the car was in fact stolen. When asked for his identification, he presented a stolen ID from a guy named Misner. He was detained and brought into custody, and his fingerprints positively identified him as Ted Bundy. He was subsequently connected and charged with the Tallahassee Sorority murders and the murder of 12-year-old Kimberly Leach.

During his trial, Bundy was examined for several hours by Dorothy Lewis, a female professor at the New York University Medical Center. She diagnosed him as a manic-depressive who committed these horrible murders while in his "depressive" phase. It was also believed that his violent sexual tendencies arose from the violent pornography that he occasionally came across when he was young.

During his interviews, he spoke often about his addiction to violent pornography, and about how his addiction grew until it got to the point where he wanted to experience it in real life. I'm not entirely sure how much of this is true, considering that pornography was much less accessible during Ted's childhood than it is today. However, in today's age, I do agree that this could be a motivating factor for a weak-minded individual to want to cause harm to another.

Once a person is "perverted," there is almost no going back, and it can be extremely difficult for them to deal with their impulses unless they are able to find a partner who is willing to partake in these out-of-the-ordinary sexual activities. They may attend long term therapy with a professional who can help them to control their compulsions. However, one must want to change in order to actually do so.

Bundy was finally put to death via electric chair on January 24, 1989. A large crowd of around five hundred people were gathered outside to celebrate the execution. They even cheered once he was officially declared dead. It was reported that many in the crowd were chanting, "Burn, Bundy, burn!"

His last meal? Nothing, he refused it. His last words were "I'd like you to give my love to my family and friends." What a classy guy. To be more realistic, his last words should have been, "I'd like to give my love to all the dead bodies out there."

Death by electric chair is actually quite interesting. It was initially implemented in the United States as a more humane method than hanging. However, it was soon discovered that it is much more brutal than was first thought. Professor and journalist Dr. Harold Hillman has studied the effects of the electric chair quite extensively. Dr. Hillman explains that the use of electricity to cause death started with veterinarians who euthanized unwanted pets. It was thought that electrocution caused instantaneous death, since the subject did not move while being killed. The first electric chair was invented in 1881 and was put to use for the first time in 1890. Dr. Harold Hillman describes the process and effects of execution via the electric chair:

> 'The metal skull-cap-shaped electrode is attached to the scalp and forehead over a sponge moistened with saline. The sponge must not be too wet, or the saline short-circuits the electric current, nor too dry, as it would then have a very high resistance. Additional curved electrodes are moistened with conductive jelly and bound to the prisoner's legs after he or she has been strapped into the chair. After the witnesses, which include doctors, have withdrawn to the observation room, the warden pulls a handle to connect the power supply. The "jolt" of 6-12 amps at 2,000—3,000 volts lasts a few seconds. The current surges and is then turned off, at which the body is seen to relax. The doctors wait a few seconds for the body to cool down, and then auscultate the heart. If it is still beating, another "jolt" is applied. The prisoner's hands grip the chair and there is a violent movement

of the limbs which may result in discoloration or fractures. The tissues swell; micturition and defecation occur; steam, or smoke rises and there is a smell of burning."

The electric chair is anything but painless. It's actually pretty impressive to see such a brutal device in use today (as of the writing of this book). However, if it is being used, it is not the sole method of execution. It serves either as a backup if another method was unable to be performed, or it can be used at the request of the condemned.

Eyewitnesses to the horrific scene of death by electric chair seem to agree that it's pretty disturbing. U.S. Supreme Court Justice William Brennan described his experience in all its gory glory:

"...the prisoner's eyeballs sometimes pop out and rest on [his] cheeks. The prisoner often defecates, urinates, and vomits blood and drool. The body turns bright red as its temperature rises, and the prisoner's flesh swells and his skin stretches to the point of breaking. Sometimes the prisoner catches fire... Witnesses hear a loud and sustained sound like bacon frying, and the sickly sweet smell of burning flesh permeates the chamber."

Ted Bundy's Medieval Punishment

Many sexual offenders back in the medieval times had either their testicles crushed or were fully castrated, testicles, shaft, and all. Another practice was the use of a tool called the "pear of anguish." This device was a pear shaped dildo device with sharp points at the end that was inserted into the orifices of the wrongdoer. It was usually inserted into the rectum, mouth, or vagina and when screwed (no pun intended), its pear-shape quartered iron leaves would slowly expand, causing excruciating pain and irreparable damage.

Rapists were also subject to the "Spanish donkey," otherwise known as the "wooden horse" treatment. This was simply a large rectangular wooden block with a very sharp triangular shaped metallic edge fixed on top. The accused is set atop of it as if they were straddling a horse while heavy weight is strung around each foot. From the weight on their feet, the person is gradually pulled down until they are sliced in half.

Now, I do like this method, considering that it takes much

more time for Bundy to die. On the other hand, another lethal option to consider would be saw torture. It's just like it sounds. Two men take a logging saw that's nearly the length of a man, and while hanging the prisoner upside down with both legs split apart, they begin to saw him in half, starting at the groin area.

This form of execution was particularly horrible because the condemned tended to survive up until the saw reached their vital organs, somewhere around mid-torso. This is because much of the victim's blood rushes to the head and upper body, so they would not have bled out as much when the sawing began. This meant that the condemned endured many rips of the saw before succumbing to death. Often, when the saw reached the abdomen, the executioners stopped, leaving the person to hang there for hours until they finally died from their wounds. After death, the executioners recommenced to saw the person until they were completely split in half.

Here is how it happens... The town magistrate orders the execution of Bundy in the middle of the town square. Finally, on this delightful day, with birds singing in the air, Bundy's happy ass is fastened to a wooden panel and drawn by horse as he is escorted through the overwhelmingly large, raging crowd. Slowly trotting his way toward the execution platform, he is struck with rocks and spat on while inching through the enormous mob.

Once atop the gallows, Bundy is tied upside down with his arms and legs spread-eagled. First, the tip of the pear of anguish is inserted into his dick hole and slowly screwed open until the head of his penis is completely spread apart and shredded. Although this was not the traditional use of this device, I think it is a well-deserved commencement of punishment. Do not fret; the pear is inserted into his anus and wrenched so wide that it destroys his colon. Subsequently, the mechanism is violently ripped out of him. Next, he is simply castrated with a dulled blade. Although this may seem life threatening, none of it is particularly lethal just yet, and lucky for Ted, as he has the hopes of living for many more hours to come.

The executioners need to take a break, so they cut Bundy down and allow him to drop onto the platform. Then, from above the gallows lowers a maniacal looking cage from a pulley system, called a gibbet.

The gibbet is an archaic iron cage crafted in the form of a human being. Their initial use was a display case for condemned prisoners who were executed. Much of the time, the executed was encapsulated in tar to be preserved in these cages forever. However, local kids often set them on fire and watched them burn for their amusement. Nevertheless, it was discovered that the gibbet could serve perfectly as a method of torture and execution as it was. Shockingly, these cages were scattered through most of medieval Europe. In fact, they were so common that locals used them as signposts for travelers. In an article written by a Scottish world traveler in *Once a Week* (1866), he describes his discovery of such a device and its indicative use:

"Quivering in agony, there she swung, the blazing sun striking fiercely on her nakedness, quickly causing a terrible thirst to rage throughout the frame, and, while yet life was strong, the fevered blood to course madly through the swollen veins. Not long before the ants, pondering over the drops of blood which fell from her spike-pierced feet, would climb in countless myriads up the old tamarind-tree, across the branches, and down over the iron bars to the fountain of this horrid feast; while mosquitoes and sandflies disputed with these and many other parasites which should suck fastest at the life and strength of a poor human creature, hung up to be eaten thus alive."

Bundy is forcefully latched inside the gibbet and hung from the gallows for the next two days. He is naked and exposed to the sweltering sun. He faces another 48 hours of stones and rotten food being thrown at him by angry townsfolk as his skin blisters and swells. After being in the scorching sun for the entirety of this time, he has an unbearable sunburn. Why quickly (or slowly) cut him in half when we have a perfectly appropriate execution by means of flaying?

Flaying was a very common execution method in many different countries during the middle ages. The prisoner's hands were tied above their head and the executioner took a typical knife, cutting deep into the skin, often starting at the face and working his way around in a very meticulous way. Flaying was like an art, and the artisan was expected to get the skin off in one piece. As you could imagine, this is excruciatingly painful, and it takes quite a long time for the flayed person to die. Usually, death occurs when the flaying reaches the waist area. However, an American pioneer and historian by the name of Silas Claiborne Turnbo recounted a story by which he was told about a man named John Mankins, who survived a full body flaying for up to one hour after his skin was fully removed by an angry band of Native American tribesmen in 1853. While interviewing an eyewitness, Turnbo learned that Mankins was guilty of cold-bloodedly murdering a Native woman for the kicks of it. In the story *Flayed Alive by Indians*, S. C. Turnbo wrote:

"A man of the name of John Mankins, formerly of Marion County, joined the other party he was a large man and bore the name of being quite over bearing and disagreeable. When he left Marion County to join the emigrants he was living in the Flippen Barrens between Yellville and White River. The two trains after starting traveled together for a while but finally they separated, often they were 10 miles apart. Before reaching the frontiers, Mankins made my boasts that he would shoot the first of the Indian race he saw; be it man, woman or child. The man repeated these threats so frequently after arriving on the frontiers that the remainder of the party grew alarmed and tried to induce him to not to do so for fear the entire party would be massacreed. Being a long headed and dont care sort of fellow he paid no attention to their advice.

Arriving at an Indian reservation, and while passing on they reached an encampment where there were only a few women and children at camp, the warriors being away on a hunt. This gave the man an oppertunity to carry his threats into execution and he willfully murdered a squaw by shooting her. The other emigrants deplored the cold blooded wicked act of the heartless man. They knew the tribe would avenge the death of the woman. They traveled on with the expectation of being attacked ever hour but they were not molested until the 4th day after the woman was killed, when the emigrant saw a band of Indians coming in pursuit. They were all mounted on ponies and numbered one hundred. Each warrior was in full war paint. The emigrants were in camp some ten miles from our train. The Indians came with a rush and without making a halt to parley surrounded the camp and demanded the murderer or they would kill and scalp all the members of the train, including women and children. The white men were well armed and had made preparation, for defense should the whole party be attacked.

On the demand of the warriors the leaders found that they were too small in number to resist the enraged Indians even if they wanted to. Mankins had committed such a wicked murder that they had no sympathy for him and they handed him over at once. The fury of the band rose to a high pitch and they informed the white men that they were going to inflict one of the most painful tortures known to the murderer. The prisnor knew he was doomed to a terrible fate and the trembling wretch begged and implored the white men to save him from the vengence of the red men, but his pleading was in vain he had brought it on himself he would have to pay the penalty that suited the desire and thirst of the warriors. The Indians took a stake (lariat) rope off of one of their ponies 60 feet long that was made from the raw hide of buffalo and bound the man head and foot; to one of the hind wheels of a wagon. The Indians did not delay much time in preliminaries when they examined their knives to see that they had keen edges and the awful scene of flaying a man alive began, they began at the neck and the mans blood was soon flowing little streams down his nude body for they had stripped him of all his clothes before they tied him to the wheel. They slowly but surely took the skin from his entire body not in small bits or strips, but whole. The awful torture was done in the presence of the white men. Mankins struggled and screamed in agony, his suffering was terrible and miserable; he begged prayed and cursed. The bloody work went on. The unbearable torture was continued. The man had cruelly murdered a poor defenseless Indian woman, and the tribe she belonged to were punishing him with the worst torture they could devise. The exultant Indians finished their horrible and painful work, and gave a yell of delight; their victim was still alive but had gradually become unconscious. They unbound him, and the bleeding, writhing form dropped to the ground where it lay quivering for an hour when death put an end to life and further cruelty by the Indians. Not an Indian left until they were satisfied he was dead; they then mounted their ponies and with war whoops they departed, carrying the human hide with them."

Another instance of this particular execution occurred in ancient Alexandria, in 415 AD. The ancient philosopher, teacher and mathematician by the name of Hypatia was subjected to this terrible fate. She was systematically killed by a group of Christian monks led by a magistrate who detested her influence in politics and affiliations with paganism. Her death was persuaded by rumors that were propagated by the archbishop, Cyril, who wanted to turn Alexandria into a Christian theocracy.

It is recorded that Hypatia was flayed alive with tiles. However, the word had a much different meaning than how we tend to use it today. Through the translations, although professionals state that the word *ostrakois* or "tiles" was used to describe roof tiles, it is also a literal term to describe oyster shells. With this discrepancy, it may be a little uncertain which of the exact tools used to murder Hypatia.

There are a couple of accounts of what happened to her, but with each account it is certain that she suffered a horrific death. From what is known, she was publicly stripped and beaten by Christian monks while being dragged through the streets of Alexandria in broad daylight. Once they arrived at a church, these monks used sharp oyster shells (or roof tiles) to flay her alive. After methodically cutting off her skin until she was dead, they mutilated her corpse and took her remains to the edge of the city to burn them atop a pyre. Ancient contemporaneous historian Socrates Scholasticus recorded her death within his writings titled *Historia Ecclesiastica*. Regarding this, he wrote:

"There was a woman at Alexandria named Hypatia, daughter of the philosopher Theon, who made such attainments in literature and science, as to far surpass all the philosophers of her own time. Having succeeded to the school of Plato and Plotinus, she explained the principles of philosophy to her auditors, many of whom came from a distance to receive her instructions. On account of the self-possession and ease of manner, which she had acquired in consequence of the cultivation of her mind, she not unfrequently appeared in public in presence of the magistrates. Neither did she feel abashed in coming to an assembly of men. For all men on account of her extraordinary dignity and virtue admired her the more. Yet

even she fell a victim to the political jealousy
which at that time prevailed. For as she had
frequent interviews with Orestes, it was
calumniously reported among the Christian
populace, that it was she who prevented
Orestes from being reconciled to the bishop.
Some of them therefore, hurried away by a
fierce and bigoted zeal, whose ringleader was
a reader named Peter, waylaid her returning
home, and dragging her from her carriage,
they took her to the church called Cæsareum,
where they completely stripped her, and then
murdered her with tiles. After tearing her
body in pieces, they took her mangled limbs to
a place called Cinaron, and there burnt them.
This affair brought not the least opprobrium,
not only upon Cyril, but also upon the whole
Alexandrian church. And surely nothing can
be farther from the spirit of Christianity than
the allowance of massacres, fights, and
transactions of that sort. This happened in the
month of March during Lent, in the fourth
year of Cyril's episcopate, under the tenth
consulate of Honorius, and the sixth of
Theodosius."

The pain experienced by Bundy through this torture would be downright unimaginable. However, I can envision what it would look like to sec him scream in terror as an executioner thrusts the sharp end of a knife into his skin, slicing deep into the middle of his forehead as he attentively cuts away in a vertical motion. He works his way around the top of Bundy's scalp down to the neck. Then he works the knife back around and runs the blade through the middle of his face, ensuring the blade is fixed underneath every layer of skin. Next, the medieval executioner takes his filthy, grimy fingernails and burrows them into the incision on the top of his head. Digging his fingers deep underneath the scalp, he takes a nice grip of each flap of skin. Then, rip and cut... rip and cut...

Chapter 7

Edmund Kemper "The Co-ed Butcher"

One side of me says, I'd like to talk to her,
date her. The other side of me says, I
wonder what her head would look like on
a stick. —Edmund Kemper

Edmund Emil Kemper III had quite an unconventional upbringing, to say the least. Born on December 18th, 1948, he was the only son and middle child of Ed Kemper Jr. and Clarnell Strandberg, neither of whom seemed to care much for him. Edmund was an extremely intelligent young man with an IQ of 136, classifying him in the "Genius" category. At the age of eight, Edmund's parents divorced, leaving him to be raised with his two sisters by only his mother.

In later interviews, Kemper said that this was when he started taking out his frustrations on animals. Apparently, his mother was a verbally abusive alcoholic who constantly put him down. He even stated that his sisters treated him in a less than loving way as well. Apparently, his older sister tried to push him into the deep end of a swimming pool when he was young, nearly drowning him. In another case, he said the same sister pushed him close to an oncoming train, almost getting him hit.

With the constant belittling and accusing from his mother and sisters of him being the cause of the family breaking apart, Kemper started to develop a deep hatred for women at an early age. When the hatred grew further, Kemper started killing cats. Studies show that when boys start killing cats early in their adolescence, it is cause for alarm that could lead to future violence against women, the reason being that cats have very feminine characteristics, and when the boy tortures and kills them, he is likely fantasizing about doing those things to a girl. Kemper buried neighborhood cats alive only to dig them up later and dissect their bodies.

Kemper noticed one day that his cat was losing interest in him and started giving his sisters more attention. At the age of thirteen, he took it up to his room, where he viciously mutilated it. As it showered blood in all directions, Kemper vigorously stabbed the cat as he tightly held its trembling body down on the bed. He took his machete and poked and sliced at the top of its head until he cut through to the brain. Once it was deceased, he cut the cat up into pieces and buried the majority of it in the backyard. The rest he saved in his closet. Once the act was done, Kemper believed that the cat would be his forever. It was his spirit animal, never to leave his side.

His mother was shocked when she found pieces of the cat in the closet. Kemper totally denied it, saying that someone else must have killed it and placed it there. In a normal household, this would be equivalent to a kid caught hording cookies; Kemper fervently denying it in a prepubescent, whiney tone. "Please believe me, I don't know how it got there, someone else must have done it, I swear."

Kemper retained the belief of spiritual marriage throughout his coed murder spree. He only killed girls whom he found attractive. He thought the only way that he could even touch them was to kill them, and that by doing so, they joined him in eternal spiritual marriage. Kemper's sister, who confirmed everything, supports this statement. When he mentioned to her that he liked his teacher, she playfully said to him, "Why don't you go and kiss her?" Kemper's response was very unsettling: he replied, "If I kiss her, I would have to kill her first."

Kemper has been quoted as saying, "When they were being killed, there wasn't anything going on in my mind except that they were going to be mine... That was the only way they could be mine." Also, while testifying in court, Kemper said, "They were like spirit wives... I still had their spirits. I still have them."

142

Kemper's mother was so emotionally abusive to him that she made him sleep in a locked, windowless basement. Apparently, she was afraid that he might rape his sisters. This experience alone can be extremely psychologically demoralizing for a boy who is starting to experience puberty. Instead of educating her son and talking to him, she demeaned and embarrassed him, further alienating him from social norms.

In 1963, Kemper couldn't handle the abuse anymore and decided to run away to live with his father. However, according to Kemper, his presence made his father's new wife very upset. She had migraines and panic attacks when he was around. I can't help but imagine that this had a lot to do with Kemper's awkwardness and anti-social tendencies. He was known to fixedly stare at others without speaking, often imparting a troubling feeling on those around him. With his already huge stature – at 15 years old, he was a towering 6' 4", 160 lbs. creepy teenager reeking of filthy socks soaked in semen – this woman must have been terrified of him. Because of this, he was shortly shipped off to his paternal grandparents to live in their farmhouse located in North Fork, California.

In the 1973 article written by Hugh Stephens, titled *I'll Show You Where I Buried the Pieces of their Bodies*, Kemper stated that his grandmother was a wretched old woman who belittled and emasculated him and his "senile" grandfather. Within the first year that Kemper lived with his grandparents, at the age of 15, he ended up violently killing both of them.

After overhearing discussions in which his grandmother spoke about sending him back to live with his father, he became angry. Although he didn't want to live with his father anymore, he also didn't want to stay with his grandparents, nor his mother. Clearly, Edmund felt like he had no options, and his rage got the best of him. When his grandmother was sitting at her typewriter, Kemper went and grabbed one of his grandfather's guns and shot her twice in the back of the head. Then he went into the kitchen and grabbed a large knife, which he used to stab her multiple times in the torso because he thought she may have been alive and he "didn't want her to suffer."

When his grandfather came home, Edmund was afraid that he would be angry at him, so after giving a generous wave to him, he shot his grandfather while he was grabbing groceries from the vehicle. Kemper said that he didn't want his grandfather to live with knowing that his wife was murdered in such a way. Soon after the murders, Kemper said that he felt overwhelming remorse and called his mother to confess. After they hung up, she called and reported it to the police, as did Kemper; and the sheriffs went on to pick Edmund up without incident.

From there, Kemper was found to be insane, and was sent to Atascadero State Hospital to carry out a four-year stay, after which he was deemed safe to be released. That's right folks, only four years. Kemper was released not because he was cured of his homicidal tendencies, but because he was incredibly intelligent and was able to manipulate the staff into thinking that he was harmless.

Upon his release in 1969, Kemper had grown to an astounding 6'9", weighing around 280 lbs. The guy was a monster, both literally and figuratively. Against the wishes of his doctors, Kemper was released into the care of his mother (in Santa Cruz, California) who remained the verbally abusive alcoholic that he remembered.

While locked away, Kemper missed the best years of his life. He missed out on high school. He could have been a huge football star. His first kiss may have been with the head cheerleader. Her head might have even remained attached. He missed out on losing his virginity on prom night with his date's detached torso. He missed out on going to the bar with his best friends on his 21st birthday. He missed out on the opportunity to develop meaningful relationships with friends and then murder them in a fit of rage. Instead, Kemper spent day and night talking with doctors and older trustees whom he had nothing in common with. When he was released, he was opened up to a world that was completely alien to him. He felt like an "old fogey," since everyone his age talked with a slang that he had never heard before.

After coming home, Kemper started to drive around his neighborhood for fun. He loved to drive. He went as far as to say that driving was his hobby. This is when he started to pick up hitchhikers. Originally, he did this for the social interaction. He wanted to work on his social skills. For this time, Kemper didn't care who he picked up; he helped people get from point A to point B, only wanting to chat with them. However, he started to develop fantasies about killing the young beautiful college girls from around the various universities in his area.

Kemper was as awkward as ever. Knowing this, he held the lingering belief that the only way he was going to be with a beautiful girl was if he killed her first. In doing so, he would be able to do whatever he wanted to her. Further, he developed even more disturbing sexual perversions. Later, he described that when he was younger, the mere act of decapitating his sisters Barbie dolls gave him an orgasm. He said, "I remember there was actually a sexual thrill... you hear that little pop and pull their heads off and hold their heads up by the hair. Whipping their heads off, their body sitting there. That'd get me off."

These perversions burned inside Kemper until he finally acted on them. Beginning his murderous campaign in 1972, Kemper started with the slaying of six beautiful young college girls, ultimately ending in 1973 with the fiendish murder of his mother and her best friend, Sally Hallett.

Mary Anne Pesce and Anita Luchese

18-year-olds Mary Anne Pesce, and Anita Luchese were Kemper's first victims. On May 5, 1972, Mary and Anita were picked up in Berkeley while hitchhiking to Stanford University to visit a friend. However, Kemper had other plans, and instead drove them to a remote cul-de-sac while holding them at gunpoint.

Kemper secured both of the girls' hands and took Anita out of the car first. He shoved her into the trunk and returned to Mary, where she was frantically struggling while handcuffed to the backseat. This is when Kemper took a plastic bag and dressed it around her head and wrapped a bathrobe belt around her neck. Pulling hard on the belt, it ripped before it did any damage to Mary. So, instead of strangling Mary, Edmund decided to pull out his knife and start stabbing. Edmund said that he was surprised at how difficult it was to kill someone this way. He said that it's not like in the movies where you stab them and they fall. He inflicted 11 stab wounds into Mary as she thrashed and flailed while he stabbed her torso and back. Eventually, Kemper cuffed her chin and violently thrust her head back before slicing her throat "from ear to ear." He said that's when she immediately lost consciousness.

Next, he went back to the trunk of the car and was faced by Anita, now desperately questioning him about the blood on his hands. He said that he punched Mary in the face for getting loud with him and she'd better go out there to help her friend. Once he successfully pulled Anita from the trunk, Edmund wildly swung the knife into her. He stabbed at her throat, eyes, and heart, eventually killing her after a series of heavy thrusts to the body.

After the deed was done, Edmund shoved the girl's corpses into his trunk and took them home with him to Alameda. Once there, he decapitated them in his bedroom and had sex with their throats. He took their headless bodies into the bathtub where he cut off the rest of their appendages with intervals taken to snap Polaroids and masturbate.

After disposing of their bodies in various areas around the county, Kemper decided to keep the heads for a while. He took them as he drove around, often masturbating with them to simulate oral sex. He eventually tossed them into a ravine after they became too decayed to enjoy anymore.

Aiko Koo

15-year-old Aiko Koo was Kemper's next victim, on September 14, 1972. Aiko was a beautiful and talented young dancer with aspirations to pursue a profession in Korean ballet. Aiko was even invited to perform in St. Louis to participate in the Worlds Trade Fair in the following weeks and she couldn't have been more excited. However, she never made it.

On her way to her dance class in San Francisco, Aiko missed the bus, so she decided to hitch a ride. After picking her up, Kemper forced her to go with him to Bonnie Doon, Santa Cruz. This is where he plugged her nose while her mouth was duct taped, smothering her until she lost consciousness. Kemper thought she was dead and pulled her out of the car to have sex with her. During intercourse, Aiko started to regain consciousness and realized what was happening. She flailed and tried to move, but Kemper "took the muffler from around her neck" and choked her with it.

After she was dead, he continued to have sex with her lifeless body. He threw her corpse in his trunk and went out for drinks. Before entering the bar, Kemper opened the trunk to make sure Aiko was dead. He sat there and admired her deceased carcass like it was a trophy. He later dismembered her body and scattered her parts throughout the county. Like his previous victims, he held on to the head for a while to use as his own personal sex toy.

During this time, Edmund was seeking the help of two psychiatrists who were interviewing him to decide whether he was harmless enough for his juvenile record to be sealed and expunged. On the day of the final interview, Kemper had Aiko's head in the trunk of his car while the ignorant psychiatrists approved the sealing of his juvenile record.

Cynthia Ann Schall

Four months later, on January 8, 1973, 19-year-old

Cynthia Ann Schall became Kemper's next victim. Edmund had just purchased a new .22 Ruger pistol and was itching to use it. He found Cindy hitching from Santa Cruz on her way to the Cabrillo college campus in Watsonville. Once in Watsonville, Kemper instructed Cynthia to get in his trunk while he held her at gunpoint. As she was getting into the trunk, Kemper shot her in the head. Kemper was very pleased with the fact that it was so easy to kill in this way, saying, "One second she's animated, the next second she's not."

Once Cindy was dead, Kemper took her to his house and mutilated her body in his bathtub while his mother was at work. He decapitated her and buried the head in his mother's garden. While placing the head, he faced it as if Cynthia were looking toward his bedroom. Kemper was quoted by saying that sometimes at night while he lay in bed, he talked to her and said "loving things" as if he were talking to a girlfriend or wife.

Rosalind Thorpe and Alice Lui

On February 5, 1973, following a heated argument with his mother, Edmund left his home livid and bloodthirsty. He was out looking for the first decent-looking girl to "blow her brains out." Early in the day, Edmund made his way to a campus in Santa Cruz where he stumbled upon Rose. After getting into his front seat, Rose and Kemper sped off, only to come across a hitchhiking Alice Lui just a little way up the street. As the trio traveled, Alice and Rose started to take notice that he wasn't taking them back to town. When Kemper detected their apprehension, he immediately pulled the vehicle over and shot Rose directly in the side of her head. Next, he aimed his gun at Alice, who was so petrified that she simply covered her face with her hands. Kemper turned to the back seat and released a hail of bullets at her, shooting her in the head and body. Kemper then started to drive again. Once they got to a secluded area, Kemper shot Alice again, point-blank in her temple. After throwing their bodies in his trunk, he couldn't wait to get them upstairs. After pulling up in front of his mother's apartment, Kemper used an ornamental sabre to cut the girls' heads off right there in the open. He dumped their bodies in Alameda County the next day.

Clarnell Strandberg

Edmund both despised and loved his mother. I believe it was these mixed emotions that led him to act out as he did against these young women. He said that he was killing his mother over and over again. Considering that he felt such a connection with these girls through death, it makes sense in a weird, sadistic sort of way. Eventually, Kemper became sick of himself and wanted to quit killing. He looked at it as an addiction that he tried to control. It was the moment of this realization that Kemper decided to kill his mother, on the night of April 21, 1973.

It was late at night when he heard Carnell sloppily walk through the door after returning home from a night of drinking. Once she had staggered into bed, she started to read a book, as she usually did before falling asleep. Edmund walked into her room, and she blurted out to him, "I suppose you're going to want to sit up all night and talk now." Like a boy who had just been scolded, he replied, "No, good night."

After sulking for a couple of hours, Edmund decided it was time. Around 5AM, he grabbed a claw hammer and returned to his mother's room, bashing her head in as she slept. While she lay there dying, Edmund grabbed a knife from the kitchen and slit her throat. Once she was finally dead, he stripped her nude and cut off her head. Then, in a way to humiliate her, he had sex with her headless corpse. After that, he put her head on the mantle and angrily lobbed darts into it as he yelled and cursed at it for hours.

Sally Hallett

After Edmund was finished mocking and mutilating his mother's corpse, he called her best friend over to the apartment. He told Sally that he wanted to take her and his mother out for an Easter dinner. Once Sally arrived at the house, Kemper came up behind her and locked his arm around her gullet. After violently lifting her up off the ground, he broke her neck. Edmund later said that he was surprised at how quick she died, but once he saw that she was just dangling by the skin of her throat, he knew she was gone. He later decapitated her and attempted to have sex with Sally's headless body.

The next day, on Easter of 1973, Edmund loaded Sally Hallett's car full of guns and ammunition and attempted to flee across country. Before leaving the house, he left a note to be discovered by the police, which read:

> "Appx. 5:15 a.m. Saturday. No need for her to suffer any more at the hands of this horrible "murderous Butcher." It was quick asleep the way I wanted it. Not sloppy and incomplete, gents. Just a "lack of time." I got things to do!!!"

As Kemper drove across the country, he closely listened to the radio for news of the grisly discovery. However, in time he became very upset that nothing was mentioned. After two days of running he decided he was going to give himself up, lest he kill more people (so he says).

Kemper's Capture and Trial

It was in Pueblo, Colorado where Edmund stopped at a phone booth to make the call to the police, not only confessing to the murders of his mother and her best friend, but also admitting to being the co-ed butcher. The police apprehended him at the phone booth without incident. Even though Edmund's stature was quite intimidating to them, knowing that at any moment he could snap their necks while being handcuffed, they took him peacefully.

Edmund Emil Kemper III's trial went as expected. He pled "not guilty by reason of insanity" and was examined by three psychologists. The trio agreed that he was sane, saying that he was just a "sadistic sex maniac." Edmund agreed with their deliberation and was sentenced to life in prison. Kemper mentioned that although he deserved prison, he would have liked very much to have gone back to the same hospital that he spent 5 years in while he was younger, saying that he could have done some very positive things to help assimilate some of the troubled patients back into society. I found it pretty disturbing and a little wacky that he could possibly think he had any kind of ability to normalize someone when he's as screwed up as he is.

Edmund Kemper's Medieval Execution

Kemper is a sick son of a bitch, literally. Although he has publicized remorse for what he has done, I do not believe a damned bit of it. Kemper is a highly intelligent, master manipulator, and I find it extremely convenient that whenever we see these serial killers finally apprehended, they suddenly have regrets and feelings of remorse. I don't buy it, and even if he is sincere in his regrets, I don't care. He deserves a medieval-style execution in the most dreadful way possible, and even Kemper himself would agree. Before sentencing, Kemper's judge asked him what he thought his punishment ought to be. Kemper said that he deserved to be tortured to death. Let's accommodate, shall we?

Kemper was extremely brazen in his actions. So brazen, in fact, that I think we would see a fair end to his miserably benighted life had he done this in medieval times. A Sicilian man by the name of Perilaüs thought of a genius execution device sometime around 600 to 554 BC. Utilizing his brilliant ingenuity and his amazing craftsmanship, Perilaüs created the brazen bull.

The brazen bull was a human roasting chamber shaped like a giant bull, made entirely of bronze. This execution mechanism was crafted in such a way as to incorporate a series of musical tubes throughout the compartment that lead to the bull's head. The condemned is placed inside the bull through a side panel, and a fire is ignited underneath the chamber. As the person screams, the contraption bellows out the sound of a raging bull and smoke steams out of the nostrils.

Not only was this device utilized to cause one of the most excruciating and agonizing deaths conceivable, but it also served as a sick form of entertainment for gathering crowds, as this execution was typically performed in public.

The brazen bull was a wicked form of punishment. What's ironic is that the artisan who crafted this nearly unimaginable execution chamber became the first person for it to be tested on. When Perilaüs presented this device to "Phalaris the tyrant" of Akragas, Sicily, Phalaris put him to death because he was so disgusted that Perilaüs had thought up such a device to be used on his own countrymen.

Even though Phalaris immensely enjoyed watching the

torture and execution of his subjects, and was impressed with the execution chamber, he basically condemned Perilaüs for treason for making it. This event was recounted by Diodorus Sicilus, a Greek non-contemporary historian. In his works, *Bibliotheca Historica*, Vol IV, later translated to English, Diodorus wrote:

"The sculptor Perilaüs made a brazen bull for Phalaris the tyrant to use in punishing his own people, but he was himself the first to make trial of that terrible form of punishment. For, in general, those who plan an evil thing aimed at others are usually snared in their own devices.

This Phalaris burned to death Perilaüs, the well-known Attic worker in bronze, in the brazen bull. Perilaüs had fashioned in bronze the contrivance of the bull, making small sounding pipes in the nostrils and fitting a door for an opening in the bull's side; and this bull he brings as a present to Phalaris. And Phalaris welcomes the man with presents and gives orders that the contrivance be dedicated to the gods. Then that worker in bronze opens the side, the evil device of treachery, and says with inhuman savagery, "If you ever wish to punish some man, O Phalaris, shut him up within the bull and lay a fire beneath it; by his groanings the bull will be thought to bellow and his cries of pain will give you pleasure as they come through the pipes in the nostrils." When Phalaris learned of this scheme, he was filled with loathing of the man and says, "Come then, Perilaüs, do you be the first to illustrate this; imitate those who will play the pipes and make clear to me the working of your device." And as soon as Perilaüs had crept in, to give an example, so he thought, of the sound of the pipes, Phalaris closes up the bull and heaps fire under it. But in order that the man's death might not pollute the work of bronze, he took him out, when half-dead, and hurled him down the cliffs. This tale about the bull is recounted by Lucian of Syria, by Diodorus, by Pindar, and countless others beside them."

I like this method of execution for Edmund. However, we have got to keep size in consideration. Edmund is massive, and without a doubt it would be extremely difficult to get him inside of this thing. Not only difficult, but damn near impossible. Near impossible. To fix this issue, there needs to be a bit of preparation...

The catherine wheel, or the breaking wheel, was a common form of torture and capital punishment throughout Europe and many other parts of the classical world and was even used up to the 18th century.

This device was used for the most monstrous of criminals (typically multiple murderers) and carried out in various ways depending on the heinousness of their crimes. This particular execution can be carried out in many different ways. In some cases, the giant wheel of a cart is set on the ground and the victim is strapped to it. With their limbs resting over the thick solid spokes, they are bashed with a heavy iron bar, breaking every limb in the body. Other times, the person is broken on a crucifix and then displayed on the wheel. Once the person is sufficiently broken, they are raised atop a platform for the birds to feast on as they lay there unable to protect themselves. Other times, the executioner straps the person's limbs to blocks and slams the wheel itself between the blocks atop of their appendages, snapping them with ease. If permitted, some would get a mercy blow, called a *Coup de Grace*. In Germany, depending on the severity of their crimes, the condemned is either to be broken from top to bottom, or from bottom to top. Top to bottom started with a death blow to the head. I'm sure you could imagine what bottom to top must have looked like. Commonly, breaking on the wheel would not be the only punishment rendered. It was frequently a precursor to another lethal finale, as in the case of a would-be assassin going by the name of Robert-François Damiens.

Convicted of attempting to kill king Louis XV, he was first mutilated with hot iron pincers and then broken on the wheel. Even his fingers and toes were crushed. After this, the executioner attempted to pull him limb from limb with four horses, one strapped to each appendage. If that wasn't enough, while he was being stretched by the horses, the executioner dropped scalding sealing wax on his open wounds and body. Unfortunately, the horses were unable to pull him apart on their own. Seeing the horses struggle, a young girl with tears flowing from her eyes cried out from the crowd, "They're hurting the poor horse!" As funny as that is, it should give you an idea of how people viewed these kinds of offenders in their day. That crying girl was more concerned for the struggling horse than the suffering of a convicted criminal. They disconnected the horses and the executioner cut off Damien's limbs the old-fashioned way. Still alive, Damien screamed obscenities as he watched his limbs being cut from his body like a butcher to beef. It was said that even after only his torso was remaining, Damien showed signs of life. This execution was not unlike a major sporting event. People traveled great distances to watch this exhibition of human savagery.

From the medieval newspaper *The General Evening Post*, dated January 1, 1757, I uncovered an article featuring a first-hand account of this horrific execution. Written by an anonymous author, it reads:

> "The Sentence passed upon Damien was executed Yesterday: he arrived at the Greve about Three in the Afternoon, staid an Hour in the Town-Hall, and was then brought to the Scaffold, where his bloody Hand was first burnt and struck off; then the red-hot Pincers and boiling Lead, &c. were applied to the Parts mentioned in the Sentence [breast, arms, legs, and thighs]; after which he was quartered. Tho' Horses were very strong and vigorous, they could not accomplish their Work after five or six attempts; so that at last permission was granted to dismember him; and even till then there were Signs of Life remaining. His Limbs

were thrown into a Fire, which continued burning at Seven this Morning."

The breaking of the "gentle giant" Kemper would be quite the daunting task for even the most experienced of executioners. It required copious amounts of stamina just to break the average man's limbs. For such an occasion, it's likely there would be the presence of an apprentice executioner needed to render some of the blows. Certainly, a senior executioner could at least get his own mother to help him out.

In the book *Year's Journey Through France and Parts of Spain*, written by Philip Thicknesse in 1778, he vividly describes watching a man being broken in France by an executioner and his mother. What shocks me most is that Philip describes the mother as expressing great joy in aiding her son to mangle a young man. He writes:

> "The miserable wretch (a young strong man) was brought in the evening, by a faint torch light, to a chapel near the place of execution, where he might have continued in prayer till midnight; but after one hour spent there, he walked steadily from the chapel to the scaffold, accompanied by his confessor, who with great

earnestness continually presented to him, and bade him kiss the crucifix he carried in his hand. After he had ascended the scaffold and turned his eyes towards heaven, he very willingly submitted to the dreadful sentence, laying himself upon his back, and extended his arms and legs over a cross, which was laid flat, and fixed fast upon the scaffold for that purpose, to which he was then securely tied by the executioner and his mother, who assisted her son, in this dreadful business. Part of the cross was cut away, in eight places, so as to leave a hollow vacancy, where the blows were to be given, which are, between the shoulder and elbow, elbow and wrist, thigh and hip, and knee and ancle. When the wretch was securely tied down, the end of a rope which was round his neck, with a running noose, was brought through a hole in, and under the scaffold; this was to give the Coup de Grace, after breaking: a Coup which relieved him, and all the agitated spectators, from an infinite degree of misery, except only, the executioner and his mother, for they both seemed to enjoy the deadly office. The blows were then given, with a heavy piece of iron, made in the form of a butcher's cleaver without an edge, and the bones of the arms, legs and thighs were broken in eight places; at each blow, the sufferer called out, Mon Dieu! without saying another word, or even uttering a single groan. During all this time, the Confessor called upon him continually to kiss the cross, and to remember how Christ, his Redeemer suffered for us. Indeed, there was infinite address, as well as piety, in the conduct of the Confessor; for he would not permit this miserable wretch to have one moment's reflexion about his bodily sufferings, while a matter of so much more importance to him was depending; but those eight blows seemed nothing to two dreadful after-claps, for the executioner then untied the body, turned his back upwards, and gave him two blows on the small of the back with the same iron weapon; and yet, even that did not put an end to the life and sufferings of the malefactor! for the finishing stroke was, after all, done by the halter, and then the body being rolled up like a bundle of old clothes, was thrown into a great fire, and consumed to ashes."

Some of Kemper's thick bones may even take multiple hits to finally shatter. This makes for an entertaining display of physical feats, human tenacity, grotesque determination, and the resolve of a driven executioner to get the job done! The meagre onlookers have an epic tale to be told at their dinner tables for generations to come.

Once Kemper's limbs are completely devastated, only held together by the skin between the broken bones, he is then crammed into the brazen bull as if he was an oversized stuffed doll forced into a shoebox. Lifting Edmund into the side panel, the executioner harshly bends and twists his appendages in any way necessary to get him to fit inside the device. This resembles someone trying to maneuver a couch through a narrowly cornered entryway. Next, all that there is for him to do is to lay within the bull as his skin liquefies. With no working appendages, he screams as the bull thunders an enchanting melody for the mob.

Chapter 8

Dennis Rader "B.T.K. Strangler"

I actually think I may be possessed with demons, I was dropped on my head as a kid. —Dennis Rader

orn in the small city of Pittsburg, Kansas on March 9, 1945, Dennis Lynn Rader grew up with his three younger brothers in a relatively normal Christian household. From what has been said about his early childhood, he was never beaten, sexually abused, or humiliated in any way (that we know of). So, one might wonder why an otherwise normal boy would manifest fantasies about tying women up to torture and have sex with them. In later interviews, Dennis said that he knew something was different about him as early as the 6th grade, when he first started to romanticize about these things.

Over the years, not only did Dennis' perversions persist, but they evolved, and he began fantasizing about strangling and killing women, too. He kept those thoughts deeply hidden for years until they eventually materialized in 1974, when he committed the first of his 10 murders at the age of 28.

Considering that Dennis Rader is such a prolific name in the many serial killer anthologies and biographies, it would be silly for me to take a stab at offering any information that has not already been heard of by most readers of true crime literature. Instead, I will focus on the interesting details and try to effectively give my armchair psychoanalysis of Rader based on my perception of the man himself through his crimes, interviews, and confessions. I can only speculate as to what Rader's actual motives were, but when I watch him speak in his interviews and see him confess in court, I feel that he's not as complex as some may lead us to think.

Although Dennis may have had unwilling sexually perverse things done to him when he was young, we may never know for sure. I find it a little hard to buy that he grew up with this distinct perversion but had no traumatic experiences to begin with. Regardless, from the way that Rader carries himself, it is obvious that his narcissism won't allow him to be a victim in the eyes of the public. Therefore, if anything truly disturbing did happen to him, he certainly would not broadcast it. Rader wants to be known as an expert stalker and predator of humans, not a damaged young boy who couldn't figure out any other way to cope as he matured.

A few years after barely graduating high school, in 1966,

Dennis joined the United States Air Force and later earned an expert Marksmanship ribbon during his service. He served four years before he was honorably discharged. Although he was never caught, while serving, Dennis often stalked women, hired prostitutes, and committed minor break-ins and burglaries. He wished to act out his looming bondage fantasy, but he was not able to convince a prostitute to go along with it. I would be willing to bet that if he was successful in persuading one to consent, he may have gotten out of hand and killed the whore. Although that scenario would be a tragedy, it is likely that in his ignorant youth, Rader would have freaked out and ended up getting himself busted. This could have saved the lives of the many victims that were soon to follow after his departure from military service.

In 1971, Dennis married Paula Dietz, who eventually birthed his two children, a son, Brian, born July 27, 1975, and a daughter, Kerri, born June 13, 1978. In later years, Kerri went on to criticize author Stephen King for portraying her father in the movie *A Good Marriage* (2014), for which King stated that Rader was the inspiration. In 2014, Kerri Rawson, then a 36-year-old Michigan resident, blasted King, stating, "He's exploiting my father's ten victims and their families."

Personally, I am not so sure she has a legitimate reason

for such an attack. Writers take inspiration from innumerable aspects of life and imagination. Considering that King is a contemporary horror writer, it would be reasonable for him to have used Rader as a reference for a fictional story in one way or another. If Kerri wants to criticize every artist who may have been inspired by the story of her father (or any other serial killer, for that matter) then she may have just found herself a new full-time job; one without benefits. Moreover, it seems that the narcissistic characteristic does not fall far from the tree. Just look how she worded that. She said, "My father's ten victims." She was giving ownership of the victims to her father. It is apparent that she thinks that just because her father is Dennis Rader, it gives her the privilege to speak on what is okay for others to use as artistic inspiration. The narcissism here is mind-blowing.

These things are wholly expected if your father is someone who has gone to great lengths not only to kill, but also to make a statement to the world through murder. Such as the case may be, it would perhaps be best to just keep your head down and accept the reality of infamy and satire. Though some may try, it is naïve to think that you are going to control how people think or how they utilize the information that they are interested in. The mere existence of this book is a case in point.

Now to prod. In January of 1974, while Paula Rader was 3 months pregnant with Kerri, Dennis committed the first in his series of massacres. Not six months before Kerri was born, he decided to go on a sexually charged murderous rampage targeting the Oteros, a Hispanic family not far from the home of his unborn daughter.

Project Little Mex

Rader had a thing for Latino women, and shortly after the Oteros moved in, Rader caught a glimpse of the matriarch in the family, Julie Otero. He immediately decided to make her one of his "projects." These projects were women whom Rader would fantasize about and sometimes stalk. Before he began acting on his homicidal impulses, Rader became efficient at following women, breaking into homes, and stealing petty items such as panties and lingerie. Therefore, when it came time for him to take it to the next level, he was already a seasoned piece of shit, sprinkled with pervert powder and baked in the Devil's asshole.

It was early on a Tuesday morning in mid-January when Rader approached the rear end of the Otero house. Scurrying about like a diseased vulture, he cut the telephone wire and waited near the back door. Peering through the windows, he noticed that Mr. Otero was home. He was not supposed to be home. Dennis' original plan was to attack when Mrs. Otero was alone with her two children. Rader started to have second thoughts. Just before he was able to make a conscious decision to either walk away or go in, 9-year-old Joseph Otero Jr. opened the back door to let the dog out. Without thought or hesitation, Dennis jumped at the opportunity and easily forced his way into the house, gun in hand.

Once inside, the family started to panic, as did Dennis. He forced them on the floor in the living room and said the first thing that came to mind. He told them that he was not there to harm them, that he was a fugitive on the run and he needed money, food, and a vehicle. The family pleaded with Dennis to take the car and whatever else he needed and let them go. Dennis looked around and noticed that the living room was a bad spot for this to be taking place (for whatever reason), so he escorted all four of the family members, Julie, Joseph Sr., Joseph Jr., and 11-year-old Josephine to one of the bedrooms.

Dennis proceeded to tie them up, alternating between holding the gun and putting it aside. Because he was so convincing that he just wanted to get out of there without harming them, the family went along with everything he said without a fight or struggle. Trying to put myself in the victim's shoes, I do not know what I would do. Making the decision to fight would guarantee the end of a life on either side. It is a huge risk: either you win and live or lose and die. If you do not fight, you may have a chance to live. These thoughts must have been racing through Mr. Otero's mind repeatedly. Even just before his hands were completely secured with the rope, Mr. Otero may have been desperately considering whether or not he should make a move on Rader.

Once the entire family's hands and feet were tied, Dennis set his attention to Mr. Otero. He placed a bag over Joseph's head and wrapped a cord around his neck. Dennis strangled Mr. Otero until he fell unconscious. Thinking that the man was dead, Dennis began to move on to Mrs. Otero. At this time, the whole family panicked and tried to wrestle free. That is when Mr. Otero regained consciousness and ripped a hole in the bag over his face. Dennis "worked quick" and grabbed a tee shirt, wrapped it around Josephs face, and tightened another bag over his head. He swiftly moved around the room and strangled Julie with a cord until she fell unconscious. He once again did not know that she had not yet been killed. He went on to strangle Josephine with a cord and placed a bag over Joseph Jr's head, asphyxiating him effortlessly.

Noting the way he chose different methods of murder

based on the gender of his victims, it is apparent that Rader received sexual pleasure only from watching females die. From the way he described killing the male family members, it's as if he was not the least bit interested in watching them die at all.

Mrs. Otero woke up. Dazed and confused, she asked what was happening. Dennis would later acknowledge to the court that at this time he was very upset. I am assuming what he meant by this is that he was caught masturbating and reacted as anyone would. While confronting Mrs. Otero, he was asked to allow her son to live. Dennis agreed and removed the bag from Joseph Jr.'s head before giving Julie the "death strangle."

After he was sure Mrs. Otero was dead, he placed another tee shirt and bag over Jr.'s head and carried him to an adjacent room. Upon returning to the original room, Rader noticed that Josephine had regained consciousness. He grabbed her and proceeded to descend into the dark basement. One can only hope to never feel the extent of terror that little Josephine must have been experiencing as she was wielded around by this monstrous ogre who'd just massacred her family. Once in the basement, Rader grabbed a noose made of some hemp rope and hanged Josephine in the northeast part of the basement. When they found her, she was wearing only a torn bra and one sock. Her remaining clothes were located at the bottom of the stairs. Once Rader knew she was dead, he masturbated on her before leaving the house. Regarding the death of Josephine, in a letter that Dennis later sent to KAKE-TV (Kansas local news), Rader said:

> "Josephine, when I hung her really turn me on; her pleading for mercy then the rope took whole, she helpless; staring at me with wide terror fill eyes the rope getting tighter-tighter."

Rader idolized other serial killers, such as David Berkowitz (The Son of Sam) and Jack the Ripper. He often compared himself to them, as if this was an admirable quality. Watching his in-court confession, he was very confident as he spoke about his exploits, showing no remorse while he explained everything in a cold and calculated manner. From the way he described one of his murder sprees, it was as though he was bragging about what he had done. Rader stated that one of his victims, Kevin Bright, whom he shot twice in the head, was lucky that he did not use his "hit-kit" to subdue him, suggesting that Kevin would not have been able to break free from his bindings otherwise. It's as if Rader was publicizing himself as the next great serial killer, using the media coverage to transform an otherwise average narcissistic underachiever into an ultra-infamous celebrity.

Project Lights Out

Nearly 3 months after the Otero massacre, Dennis struck again. To his delight, this murder officially classified him as a stone cold serial killer. Kathryn Bright was one of his projects, and on April 4, 1974, Dennis made his move. Rader had caught a glimpse of Kathryn one day while on his way to eat lunch with his wife. He later said that she had "a pretty good figure," and immediately considered her as a potential victim. Subsequently, Dennis "trolled" and stalked her for weeks, eventually making his way inside her house on that ghastly day.

On the date of the murder, Dennis was already privy to Kathryn's schedule, so he chose a time to break into her house when he knew that she would not be home. He broke through the glass window of the back door and made his way inside where he waited for her in a bedroom, with his Colt .22 pistol in hand.

Moments later, Rader heard the front door open as Kevin and Kathryn came home. Dennis immediately confronted them; he told them the same story that he'd told the Oteros:

he was a fugitive on the run and all he needed was money and a car. However, Rader realized a crucial mistake that he had made in his haste. He'd forgotten his hit-kit. Forcing the two siblings into a bedroom, Dennis then began to rummage through the dressers for whatever he could find. He desperately pulled out anything he could use, including pantyhose, handkerchiefs, and tee shirts. Tossing the items at Kevin, Dennis instructed him to tie Kathryn's hands together. He did, and Rader next took them to an adjacent bedroom where he bound Kevin's hands and feet after having him lie on the bed.

After he secured Kevin, Rader took Kathryn into another room in the house and tied her to a chair. Learning from his previous murder, he did not want to kill them in the same room. Remembering the way that the Oteros had wailed and thrashed, he didn't want to make it that much more difficult for him to get off and enjoy the moment.

Rader decided to take care of Kevin first. He was bound, with his feet strapped to the bedframe, and Dennis wrapped a pair of panty hose around the man's neck. Upon realizing that his life was about to be snuffed out, Kevin fought with everything he had. Hands tied, he broke the makeshift bindings and scrambled to hurt Dennis in any way that he could. Rader knew that he was in trouble and decided to end things immediately. He pulled out his .22 caliber pistol and blasted a single shot, hitting Kevin in the head. Kevin dropped to the floor. Dennis was convinced that he was dead.

Rader went back to Kathryn, who was now rampaging and violently trying to escape from her bindings. Dennis instructed her to relax, but she kept asking what happened to her brother as she continued to struggle with the bindings. He made a half-witted attempt to convince her that he only injured her brother and that she needed to take him to the hospital after he left. Kathryn was not buying any of it.

Thinking that this situation could get bad very fast if Kevin actually was still alive, Rader returned to the adjacent room to make sure that he was dead. After kicking Kevin, the man sprang up and started fighting again. This time, he'd broken the restraints from his hands. While fighting over the gun, Rader was able to shoot Kevin in the head once more. Kevin dropped and now Rader was certain that he was dead.

Dennis went back for Kathryn and lunged for her neck. This must have filled her with an incredible strength initiated by her natural will to survive. She broke free from the restraints and the fight was on. Kathryn was fighting for her life and giving Dennis a good beating too. Thinking there was a chance he could be in some actual trouble, Dennis took out his knife and clumsily stabbed at the woman. He stabbed at her back, gut, and lungs, and after what seemed like forever to him, Kathryn eventually dropped to the floor. It was then that Dennis heard a noise from outside and frantically looked around the house. He noticed that the front door was open. Kevin had escaped. Rader, now drenched in both Kathryn and Kevin's blood, hastily made his way to their car to make his getaway.

Project Blackout

Dennis decided to take a leave from killing while he let his previously bungled project turn cold. It was not until three years later when he celebrated his 1977 St. Patrick's Day with another execution project.

Rader dressed up that day in the way that he imagined a police detective dressed. Chino slacks and a blazer with a briefcase (hit-kit) in hand. Rader had numerous projects planned out, just in case anything interfered with his original plan. As he walked up Hydraulic Street, Dennis noticed a boy trotting along the sidewalk with a can of soup in his hands. Dennis approached the kid, flashing him a picture of his own wife and children. Dennis said that he was a detective and needed information on where he could locate the family, asking the boy if he'd ever seen them. Five-year-old Steven said, "No," and headed home. Rader kept an eye on him as he walked into his house with the can of soup.

Dennis continued with his original project, but when he knocked on the door, no one answered. Springing at the opportunity, Rader decided to go with the new target that had just materialized before him, little Steven's house.

Dennis calmly walked to the house and knocked on the door. Steven hastily answered. Rader, now filled with adrenaline, pushed through it, declaring that he was a detective. Once inside, Rader shut the door and pulled his gun. Shirley Vian stood there in her bathrobe along with her 3 children who were sick with the flu. She yelled out, "Don't hurt us!" Attempting to temper any potential fighting spirit, Dennis told Shirley that he was not going to hurt anyone. He said that he merely had worrying sexual tendencies, and that he only wanted to tie Shirley up and have sex with her. Then the phone began to obnoxiously ring, ring, ring... Shirley said that she had friends calling to check up on her. Dennis told her not to touch the phone. He tied up her children, Steven and his two siblings, 4-year-old Stephanie and 8-year-old Bud. He led the kids to the bathroom, where he secured the door from the outside with cords and a bed. Attempting to stop the children from shouting and crying, Rader threw in random toys and a blanket that he'd found throughout the house. It's as if he thought of the children as house pets, like he was merely putting puppies in a cage. As if they would be perfectly calm and compliant, so long as they had a blanket and a toy. This remarkably ignorant inkling alone shows just how disconnected Rader truly is.

Shirley sparked a cigarette and Dennis sat and talked with her a bit. He explained to her that although the pending experience would not be pleasant, she would live. After she finished her cigarette, Rader laid her on the bed and hog-tied her in such a way that if she were to struggle, the bindings tightened around her neck. Shirley threw up on herself. Oddly, Rader attempted to comfort her and brought her a glass of water. With the phone ringing, Rader gradually became more irritated, thinking that the caller may show up at the house. For this reason, Rader moved fast. The kids relentlessly pounded on the door and screamed at Rader. Flustered, Rader took a plastic bag out of his hit-kit and placed it over Shirley's head. He took a cord and pulled it tightly around her neck, swiftly killing the young single mother. Rader wanted to kill the children, as well, but there was too much commotion going on so he decided to get the hell out of there.

Project Fox Hunt

While trolling a mid-income Wichita neighborhood, Rader noticed the beautiful, 25-year-old Nancy Fox as she was entering her duplex. From there, Rader initiated the next sequence in his game: stalking.

Rader had a specific sequence which he strictly followed as he took on each project. When later asked about this by the judge at the time of his confession, Rader stated:

> "If you've read much about serial killers, they go through what you call different phases. That's one of the phases they go through as a trolling stage. Basically, you're looking for a victim at that time. You can be trolling for months or years but once you lock in on a certain person, you become stalking. And that might be several of them, but you really hone in on that person. They basically become the...it's, that's the victim."

Shortly into the stalking phase, Rader returned to Nancy's

apartment and searched through her mail to get her name. Rader stalked Nancy to her place of work at a local jewelry store. He even went as far as purchasing items from the store in order to get a closer look at her. Rader appreciated the way that Nancy so meticulously tended to her appearance.

The more Dennis learned about Nancy, the more comfortable he became with executing the project, and on December 8, 1977, Dennis decided he would go through with it. He took his wife's car to Nancy's neighborhood and parked 2-3 blocks away from her home. He took his hit-kit along with him as he walked to the apartment. He knocked on her door, but she wasn't home. After knocking on a neighboring door, Rader realized that the other wing of the duplex was vacant. Discovering this was very gratifying for Rader. He would be able to break in to her apartment and take advantage of Nancy without anyone hearing her scream. Rader cut Nancy's phone lines and broke a window to gain entrance.

Consequent to inspecting her home, Rader noticed that Nancy cared for her apartment as well as she did herself. Everything was kept meticulously clean and orderly. This was something that Rader again had much appreciation for. Without a moment to prepare, Nancy walked through the door.

Rader immediately pulled his gun, but to his surprise, Nancy was seemingly unaffected. She told him to get out of her house and that she was calling the police, calmly walking past him and grabbing the phone. Rader told her that the phone was dead and she had no choice; she was going to have to do what he said. Nancy then realized the gravity of the situation. Rader told her that he only wanted sex and that she would be fine so long as she did everything that he told her.

Nancy removed her jacket, neatly folded it, and lit a cigarette. She said, "Let's get this over with so I can call the police." Rader gladly agreed. First, though, she needed to go to the bathroom. After inspecting it, Rader allowed her to go, telling her to come out with most of her clothes off.

Minutes later, Nancy exited the bathroom without her pants on. Rader hurriedly handcuffed her wrists behind her back. Nancy disapprovingly argued with Rader. Caught in the moment, Rader was unconcerned with what she was saying. He laid her on the bed and took his belt to her neck, pulling tight until she lost consciousness. Moments later, Nancy woke up, and Rader took this opportunity to taunt her. Whispering in her ear, he said, "I'm BTK." Nancy's eyes widened as she now began to desperately struggle and squirm. Movement was futile with Rader on top of her body. He again wrapped his belt around her neck, violently pulling until she was dead. Rader masturbated on her bathrobe before leaving.

Project Cookie

Nearly 8 years after Rader's last slaying, he committed yet another murder, on April 26, 1985. This time, his target was an easy victim, one he was already familiar with and one who he knew would be the least likely to put up much of a fight. Marine Hedge was a 5'0, 100lb recent widow who lived only 6 doors from the Rader home.

Considering that 53-year-old Marine was such a close neighbor to Rader, he cleverly executed an alibi for himself, just in case some investigator came snooping around his block asking questions. Rader timed her murder to occur on a night that he would be camping at his sons' Boy Scouts outing, nearly 200 miles from his house.

Since Dennis knew that Marine came home from work around 12 AM, he planned accordingly. Late in the night, Rader told his fellow camp chaperones that he was not feeling well and was turning in early. After going off to his tent, Rader put his plan into action. He gathered the necessary belongings and crept around to his car. After driving a while, he stopped to change his clothes and grabbed his hit-kit, which now masqueraded as a bowling bag.

Rader drove to a bowling alley, where he splashed beer on himself as if it were cologne. He called a taxi service to take him near the neighborhood. Rader portrayed himself as the average drunk who just needed a ride home. He did this so that if the driver was questioned, he would have just said that he'd dropped off some sloppy drunkard from the bowling alley. This was while Rader was supposedly sleeping in his tent nearly 200 miles away. His alibi was flawless.

Rader was dropped off a couple blocks from his home and walked the rest of the way to Marine's house. He cut through a park and the surrounding houses before strategically making his way directly to her backyard.

Upon his arrival, to Rader's dismay, he noticed that Marine's car was parked in the driveway. He had specifically showed up before 12AM so he could surprise Marine after she came home from work. With this revelation, Dennis nonetheless continued with his plan. He cut the telephone line and quietly broke into her house after wedging a door open with a screwdriver.

After a brief sweep of the house, Dennis realized that Marine was not home. Then he heard a commotion outside and discerned that Marine was approaching the front door with a male friend. Dennis scurried into her bedroom closet where he hid and salivated while she and her company chatted for a bit.

Marine's friend left, and at around 1AM, Rader emerged from the closet. Rader later explained that he'd had his belt already wrapped around her neck before she even woke up. After strangling Marine to death, he wrapped her in blankets and loaded her into the trunk of her own car. He drove to his local Christ Lutheran Church where he snapped Polaroids of Marine's lifeless body while posing her in various sex positions as he masturbated on her. Soon after, Dennis carelessly discarded her naked corpse in a ditch that was commonly used as a local dump. Dennis was a shitty neighbor.

Project Piano

After another year of hibernation, Rader attacked again. This time, it was a local Wichita mother of two, 28-year-old Vicki Wegerle. After trolling another random neighborhood, Rader caught glimpse of the beautiful young blonde-haired woman. After, he decidedly began his stalking phase. Rader regularly watched her house. Many times, he could hear her playing the piano, which is why he noted her as *project piano*.

After a period of about three weeks of planning and stalking, Dennis moved forward with his plan. He created yet another disguise which he would use to trick Vicki into allowing him inside her home, as a telephone technician. On September 16, 1986, Rader wore a yellow hardhat with a telephone company logo that he'd pasted on the front of it as he strolled Vicki's block with his hit-kit briefcase in hand. After entering various homes, pretending to inspect her neighbors' telephone connections, he eventually made his way to Vicki's door.

Passing himself off as a legitimate repairman, Vicki reluctantly agreed to allow Dennis to enter her home. Once inside, he initiated small talk as he pulled out a makeshift mechanism that he passed off as some sort of device used to test landlines. After finding that the coast was clear and that Vicki's husband was not home, he pulled out the gun from his briefcase. Vicki immediately started to cry, telling Rader that her husband would be home soon and that he had better leave. Not believing her, Rader instructed her to go to the bedroom.

Eager to use his new and improved tools, after binding her hands and feet, Rader pulled out his newly fashioned garrote.

It was made of strong, leather shoelaces with knots tied at each end for better gripping. He wrapped them around Vicki's throat and began to pull. Even so, the bindings around her hands loosened as she struggled, and she got free. Now fighting her, Rader relentlessly punched Vicki in the face as she gouged and clawed at his eyes and neck. Eventually, Rader got the upper hand. With the little time he had, he found some pantyhose in a nearby dresser, which he used to strangle Vicki to death. Rader was now convinced that there was some truth to the claim that her husband would be coming home soon. In a hurry, Rader positioned Vicki's body in various sexual positions and snapped some Polaroids before stealing her car to make his getaway.

Project Dog-side

Delores was a sweet and loving grandmother who would be yet another person who just happened to be outside at the wrong time. She was yet another victim who Rader chanced to see while trolling the Wichita neighborhoods nearly 5 years after his last slaying. Dennis decided to plan the murder to take place on January 18, 1991, while he would be out on another Boy Scouts' camping trip; this was his alibi. He labeled her *Project Dog-side* after spotting a dog kennel near her home.

After showing up early to the campgrounds, Dennis began setting up camp, long before anyone had shown up. After half-heartedly preparing the grounds, Rader left to execute his project. His plan, upon returning, was to say that he'd run out of supplies and had to make a trip to the store.

Since the Boy Scout brigade was organized out of a local Baptist church, Dennis decided that this would be his jumping off point, since he now had the keys to the doors. Once there, he was not far from Dolores' home. After changing his clothes and preparing his hit-kit, Dennis walked through the near-freezing weather toward his objective.

Once Dennis arrived at her house, he peered into Dolores' windows to catch a glimpse of her reading in bed. Seeing that there was no man in the house, Dennis made an abrupt move. He grabbed a large rock from the backyard and destroyed the large glass sliding door. Startling Dolores, she jumped up and confronted Rader. She thought that he ran his car into her house, but Rader, now wearing panty hose over his head, instructed Dolores to enter her bedroom. He told her the same thing he'd told the Oteros and the Brights, that he was wanted, and so long as she did as he told her, she would be fine.

Once bound and sprawled on her bed, Rader continued

with his lie. He assured her that he was leaving soon. Dolores told him that someone was on the way to her house and so he'd better leave now. Deciding he didn't want to risk the chance of being caught, he hurriedly ripped the panty hose off his face and wrapped it around his hands as to fashion a garrote. Seeing this, Dolores panicked, and Rader attacked. As with his other murders, once it was done, he took Dolores' body and put her in the trunk of her own car and made his escape, later to pose her dead body while he masturbated and took pictures.

Rader's Capture

In 2004, the anniversary of the Otero murders reignited talks about the BTK killer and his elusiveness. This got Rader moving again, wanting to bask in his infamy. He started sending letters to news stations and taunting police with packages that he dropped off at random locations. However, his games didn't last long. Rader made an amateur mistake. He sent in a floppy disk to test anonymous communications with investigators, but it backfired. They simply went into the disk and read the "properties" section. The disk was shown to have been saved by a man named Dennis, and it was last used at Christ Lutheran Church, where Dennis Rader just so happened to be the president of the congregation.

Dennis Rader's Medieval Punishment

Taking into account the method of murder that Rader inflicted upon his victims, one could easily imagine the common execution by hanging until he is dead. However, hanging is far too humane for this grotesque monster. We must eradicate him in a monstrous way. There is one method in particular that I am *drawn* to that is especially fitting for Rader.

Being drawn, hanged, and quartered dates as far back as 1241, and was regularly performed as a means of execution by England for the worst of perpetrators. However, in 1283, it was solely implemented for crimes of treason. This execution is commonly regarded as one of the most barbaric ways to die.

There have been hundreds of men that were executed in this way, but none with more infamy than the case of Sir William Wallace of Scotland. William Wallace was knighted "Guardian of Scotland" after successfully defeating an English army at the Battle of Stirling Bridge in 1297. This was just one year after King Edward I imprisoned the king of Scotland in an attempt to conquer their lands. However, Wallace's victory was short lived. His army was subsequently defeated at the Battle of Falkirk in 1298, and Wallace was on the run from his relentless enemies for nearly seven years. On August 3, 1305, Wallace was captured by a Scottish baron by the name of Sir John Menteith. John blamed Wallace for the death of his beloved nephew, who had died while fighting at the side of Wallace at the Battle of Falkirk. On August 23, William Wallace was paraded through the streets of London before hastily being tried. He was subsequently drawn, hanged, and quartered after a brief trial. His body parts were distributed throughout Berwick, Newcastle, Aberdeen, and Perth. His head was even displayed atop the London Bridge. There have been many successful pieces inspired by the life of Wallace. One of these is an epic poem written by a 15th century man by the name of Blind Hary, called *The Wallace*. Another is the 1995 award-winning film *Braveheart*, directed by and starring Mel Gibson.

John Reuben Davies' article, *The Execution of William Wallace: The Earliest Account*, gives us an impression of the times. Using translations of the pipe rolls from the empire of Edward I, Davies suggests that Wallace was a celebrity super villain to the English people. Even the exchequer – who otherwise inserted vague descriptions pertaining to executions – gave a semi-detailed description of the execution of Wallace. This shows us that Wallace's death had a highly significant impact on English society at the time. To clarify, the pipe rolls that Davies studied are documents that describe the costs incurred through the daily duties of the monarchy. These costs are logged and accounted for, including the cost of executions, and in particular, the traveling fees for those who placed Wallace's appendages in these various locations, Davies translates:

> "Citizens of London John of Lincoln and Roger of Paris for the same citizens render account [etc.] As expenses and payments made by the same sheriffs for William Wallace, as a robber, a public traitor, an outlaw, an enemy and rebel against the king, who in contempt of the king had, throughout Scotland, falsely sought to call himself king of Scotland, and slew the king's officials in Scotland, and also as an enemy led an army against the king, by sentence of the king's court at Westminster being drawn, hanged, beheaded, his entrails burned, and his body quartered, whose four parts were dispatched to the four principal towns of Scotland. This year, 61 shillings 10 pence."

From the book *The History of English Law Before the Time of Edward I,* (Volume II, 1898) by Sir Frederick Pollock and Frederic William Maitland, can be read:

"So Wallace was drawn for treason, hanged for robbery and homicide, disemboweled for sacrilege, beheaded as an outlaw and quartered for divers depredations."

A more detailed account of his execution comes to us from the 13th century writings *Flores Historiarum*, attributed to a controversial man referred to as Matthew of Westminster, translated and published in 1890:

"Wilielmus Waleis, a man void of pity, a robber given to sacrilege, arson and homicide, more hardened in cruelty than Herod, more raging in madness than Nero... was condemned to a most cruel but justly deserved death. He was drawn through the streets of London at the tails of horses, until he reached a gallows of unusual height, especially prepared for him; there he was suspended by a halter; but taken down while yet alive, he was mutilated, his bowels torn out and burned in a fire, his head then cut off, his body divided into four, and his quarters transmitted to four principal parts of Scotland. Behold the end of the merciless man, who himself perished without mercy!"

The first phase, drawing, was carried out in various ways depending on the severity of the crime. Conversely, many times, the condemned incurred lashes to their back before they were to be strapped face up to a fence-like wooden platform. Other times, hot iron tongs or pincers were used to rip the skin from the doomed man's chest, arms, and thighs while he approached the scaffold. Spectators threw rotten food at the prisoner, spit on him, and laughed as he was trampled or kicked by the transporting horse. Imagining Rader being dragged through the muddy streets of medieval England while being bombarded with rotten cabbage and kicked in the head by a horse puts a wicked smile on my face.

By the time Rader arrives at the gallows, he is already in pretty bad shape. He is laid onto a platform by which he is able to be hung without otherwise breaking his neck from the fall as would happen in a traditional hanging. A noose is tightly secured around his neck, and while he is strapped down, it is pulled until he loses consciousness. Then, Rader is revived and tormented again as he is strangled repeatedly, until the crowds laughter is exhausted.

Thereafter, the mutilation commences. After removing the rope from Rader's neck, the executioner has the joyous opportunity to use his favorite knife to completely remove Rader's penis and testicles. This was typically done to humiliate the prisoner. Next, the executioner slices into his belly and yanks out Rader's entrails. Again, it depends on the severity of the crimes, but in cases of extreme cruelty, the condemned could have their innards burnt as they were removed. Mind you, this was done while they were alive. Further, this would be so much more horrifying for someone like Rader, who is as narcissistic as they come. Viewing his own body as it is methodically desecrated would duly be – without a doubt – a devastating and terrifying end for such an inhumane brute as he. With still a twinkle left in his eyes, the sloppy executioner's giant axe comes down on neck. He is finally butchered in front of the pleased crowd; all limbs chopped from his torso with heavy sluggish hits.

Chapter 9

David Berkowitz "The Son of Sam"

*I didn't want to hurt them, I only wanted
to kill them. —David Berkowitz*

Also known as the ".44 Caliber Killer," David Berkowitz was born in 1953 in Brooklyn, New York. His mother, Betty Broder, was a poor Jewish woman married to an Italian man named Tony Falco. The two ran a fishery together, but they split up and started seeing other people before David was born.

David was not born until after his mother had met a successful real estate agent named Joseph Kleinman, and so he was born illegitimately. However, when his mother explained to Kleinman that she was pregnant, he threatened to leave her if she kept the baby. Therefore, she ended up giving David her previous husband's name, "Falco," and put him up for adoption. Subsequently, Pearl and Nathan Berkowitz adopted him. They were a typical middle-aged Jewish couple with lots of love to offer. Although they did not keep it from David that he was an adopted child, they told him that his actual mother died during childbirth. As a result, David blamed himself for causing his mother's death.

David was a normal kid until a series of unfortunate accidents occurred when he was very young. David actually suffered from multiple, separate head injuries. The first injury was sustained when he was only four years old. A kid dropped a large rock from the top of a building directly onto David's head. A car also hit him at the age of seven. Following this accident, he became increasingly hyperactive and unpredictably moody. He lost interest in school and put the title of petty thief and pyromaniac on his résumé at an early age. David also started killing animals and torturing bugs for fun. Although he was a juvenile delinquent, he never got into any serious trouble with the law.

Unfortunately, Pearl died of breast cancer when David was 14. As is typical with adopted children, he was extremely close with her. Some might even say too close. With Pearl gone, David neurotically blamed himself for both of his mothers' deaths. His adoptive father was not supportive, and he moved on right after Pearl's death. This infuriated David, and he hated his father's new girlfriend.

At the age of 18, David joined the U.S. Army. This is where David learned how to shoot a gun. Although he did not see any combat, David was actually an impressive marksman. While stationed in Korea, he may have lost his virginity, but this is questionable. If he did, it would be the last time he got to have sex. While in Korea, David also experimented with many recreational drugs. He dropped LSD, smoked loads of marijuana, and sniffed mounds of cocaine. Consequently, David became quite the hippy. He talked of peace and love, and at one point even refused to carry a firearm. Considering that he was still in the Army, they reprimanded him for this.

In 1971, three years after joining the military, David moved back home to New York City after an honorable discharge. When he got back, David constantly rambled about war pigs and Jesus Christ. He was now a left wing anti-war extremist and a die-hard Christian evangelist. His close friends and adopted father could not deal with his obnoxious ramblings, and David soon found himself very lonely.

He decided to look up his biological mother's records and soon found out that he was a love child born out of wedlock. This discovery overwhelmingly disturbed Berkowitz so much that it drove him mad. He considered his entire life to have been a sham and could not emotionally manage the thought of it. However, he reached out to his mother, and actually met up with her. Yet, since he had already burned his own ethereal image of her into his psyche, he was extremely disappointed with who she actually was. He nearly expected to meet an angel, and what he got was a loud-mouthed, annoying little Jewish woman.

This is when the chaos began. Nevertheless, considering that David had already known that he was an adopted child, I wonder what he'd thought he would find out. Was his adoptive circumstance that much of a shock to him? His expectations of an illustrious mother are as ridiculous as thinking that a mythical stork conceived him.

With his intense anger now directed at society, David became violent and dedicated his life to murder and mayhem. His murder spree began in the mid-1970s. After a botched attack with a knife, he began using a Charter Arms, Bulldog .44 special five-round revolver. This gun was one of the top-selling guns at the time. With it, he went on a killing spree throughout Queens, Brooklyn, and the Bronx. He simply gunned down unsuspecting victims out of nowhere, totally unprovoked.

His first shooting was in July of 1976. He approached 18-

year-old Donna Lauria and 19-year-old Jody Valenti sitting in a car around 1 AM. Just as Donna was stepping out, David drew his gun and opened fire. David killed Donna and wounded Jody. He immediately put his gun away and ran off without saying a single word. Unfortunately, Jody could not even give a proper description of the perpetrator other than that he was a stocky white male with curly hair.

With a growing number of attacks, police began to notice a pattern in the recent murders. They noticed a string of incidents that often occurred at night, happening near specific locations such as bars and lingerie stores. The shooter also seemed to target young women with long wavy dark hair. Police were also able to identify the bullets used, linking these series of murders to a single .44 special caliber revolver. They were horrified to conclude that there was a lone maniac out on their streets. Regardless, nobody was able to tie David to any of the murders.

The slayings continued throughout the years of 1976 and 1977, and Berkowitz had the entire city of New York in a panic. Young, dark-haired women were so terrified of being the next victim that they began dyeing their hair so they wouldn't be targeted.

David got cocky and began leaving letters behind, taunting police and investigators, proclaiming himself "Son of Sam." Below is an excerpt from one of his letters:

"I am deeply hurt by your calling me a woman hater. I am not. But I am a monster. I am the "Son of Sam." I am a little "brat". When father Sam gets drunk he gets mean. He beats his family. Sometimes he ties me up to the back of the house. Other times he locks me in the garage. Sam loves to drink blood. "Go out and kill" commands father Sam. Behind our house some rest. Mostly young — raped and slaughtered — their blood drained — just bones now. Papa Sam keeps me locked in the attic, too. I can't get out but I look out the attic window and watch the world go by. I feel like an outsider. I am on a different wave length then everybody else — programmed to kill. However, to stop me you must kill me. Attention all police: Shoot me first — shoot to kill or else. Keep out of my way or you will die! Papa Sam is old now. He needs some blood to preserve his youth. He has had too many heart attacks. Too many heart attacks. "Ugh, me hoot it hurts sonny boy." I miss my pretty princess most of all. She's resting in our ladies house but I'll see her soon. I am the "Monster" — "Beelzebub" — the "Chubby Behemouth." I love to hunt. Prowling the streets looking for fair game — tasty meat. The wemon of Queens are z prettyist of all. I must be the water they drink. I live for the hunt — my life. Blood for papa. Mr. Borrelli, sir, I dont want to kill anymore no sir, no more but I must, "honour thy father." I want to make love to the world. I love people. I don't belong on Earth. Return me to yahoos. To the people of Queens, I love you. And I wa want to wish all of you a happy Easter. May God bless you in this life and in the next and for now I say goodbye and goodnight. Police — Let me haunt you with these words; I'll be back! I'll be back! To be interrrpreted as — bang, bang, bang, bank, bang — ugh!! Yours in murder Mr. Monster"

At first, police began to think he could possibly have been a person of Scottish descent due to the style of writing. Police also believed that the killer was blaming a dark-haired nurse for his father's death, because two of his previous victims were studying to be nurses. The mainstream media became aware of the killer's fondness for the attention that he was getting, and investigators believed him to be a psychoneurotic with "paranoid schizophrenic delusions" due to his statements of demonic possession. Police also investigated about 56 owners of the same .44 special Charter Arms Bulldog revolver throughout the city in an attempt to match ballistics, but they came up with nothing.

Throughout 1976 and 1977, the mysterious letters continued, and so did the murders. A young couple was sitting in their motor vehicle in the early hours of the morning of October 23, 1976 when all of a sudden, gunshots blasted through their windows, striking only the driver. 20-year-old David Denaro was hit in the back of the head. Apparently, Berkowitz had mistaken Denaro for a woman due to his long hair. Luckily, Denaro survived but had to have a metal plate fitted in his skull to replace his shattered cranium. Neither of them had actually seen David, but other people in the nearby area claimed to have witnessed the same stocky, curly dark-haired man, fleeing the area on foot.

After a little more time, on April 16, 1977, David successfully committed the double homicide that he was trying for, killing both 18-year-old Valentina Suriani and 20-year-old

Alexander Esau. After Berkowitz had fatally shot the both of them in the head, he left yet another note, taunting investigators.

Similarly, a young couple was sitting in their car making out, when a man came out of nowhere and began blasting his .44 at them. He shot them both in their heads. The female, Stacy Moskowitz, died later in the hospital, but the male, Robert Violante, survived with the loss of an eye, retaining only part of his vision in the other. A man that was parked three cars ahead of the victims caught a clear glimpse of David in the streetlight, also describing him as a stocky, shaggy-haired man. This was David's most incriminating witness during the trial. He claimed that David's hair looked like a wig, and another eyewitness said the same thing: that it looked like he was wearing a "dark nylon wig." David did not have good hair!

Berkowitz' Capture

After six murders, David was eventually detained when witnesses identified his 1970 Ford Galaxy as the car seen fleeing multiple incidents. Although only a partial license plate number was seen, police were able to track him. Once David's car was located, police recovered a rifle from the back seat along with a duffel bag full of ammunition. They also found a brown paper bag that contained a .44 Bulldog revolver, which later turned out to be the murder weapon. You can only imagine the relief investigators felt with so much damning evidence at their immediate disposal.

When police finally searched David's small apartment, they found it to be an absolute mess, with psychotic graffiti spray painted on the walls. Just think back to the cliché serial killer's bachelor pads in all the second-rate murder mystery movies you have ever seen, and you will have a good visual of what this must have looked like. It just so happens that David did not bring any women home...

Among the piles of incriminating evidence, police discovered numerous implicating notebooks. They detailed over 1,400 arsons that David claimed to have committed since he was 21 years old. It would be safe to assume that David is the original inspiration for the typical psycho killer cliché seen on television shows. If you were planning to visit his apartment, his address was changed to prevent any publicity or notoriety.

Subsequently, lawmakers introduced the "Son of Sam law," which prevented famous killers from gaining publicity and profiting from their crimes. Although I am not so sure that the publicity part is working very well, considering how many subsequent killers have become quite infamous, respectively.

After dragging David into the interrogation room, he confessed to the crimes. It only took interrogators 30 minutes to break him. During the questioning, David claimed that his neighbor's dog instructed him to kill. He explained that an ancient demon that drank the blood of young girls possessed the dog. David also said he tried to kill the demon dog but was unable to due to a "spiritual interference."

Subsequently, David was convicted and sentenced to 25 years to life for each murder. Initially, he went to an insane asylum, but soon after, he was transferred to a number of other prisons, including both Sing Sing and Attica.

While in Attica, in 1979, a fellow inmate nearly killed David by cutting his throat. He did not identify his attacker. However, he did say it was a member of a satanic cult where he once congregated. This was David's new shtick. He retracted his original demonic dog claim and alleged that his murder spree was the bidding of a satanic cult called "The Process." David said that he was only one of many people responsible for the shootings. He said that he took the blame for the murders because he was a soldier and that is what he was supposed to do.

In later years, David claimed to have finally become a "born-again Christian." He changed his name from "Son of Sam" to the "Son of Hope." To this very day, he languishes in Sullivan Correctional Facility in Fallsburg, New York.

David Berkowitz' Medieval Punishment

Had he been convicted in medieval times, it could certainly be a fitting punishment for David to undergo death by a thousand cuts, otherwise known as ling chi. This ancient Chinese form of execution was traditionally reserved for murderers, traitors, and blasphemers. It was practiced from around the 10th century up to 1905. Considering this form of capital punishment was in use after the commercial release of photography (in 1839), you are easily able to find authentic pictures of what this punishment looked like. After personally viewing these pictures, I noticed a disgusted look on the executioners' faces. It appears that this was far too barbaric for even them to bear.

What happens is this: the accused is publicly stripped naked and tied to a wooden frame. The executioner makes small cuts with a common knife to the chest, arms, and legs; slowly and systematically removing body parts until the person dies, or, if the executioner happened to be in a merciful mood that day, they could decapitate the condemned or stab them in the heart. Crows and other wildlife later feasted on the abandoned corpse.

It is uncertain how long this torture lasted, since the sources vary depending on the executioner. It is said that twelve large cuts, taking as long as an hour, could be enough to get the job done. Certainly, this can be stretched over a vastly longer duration with anywhere from 100 to 3000 tiny cuts. However, you have to find the right kind of executioner to do the task properly.

As you can see, this would be a great punishment for Mr. Berkowitz. However, there are too many variables that make me want to drop this method altogether. This process has no consistency. A sympathetic, antsy, or bribed executioner could start by decapitating Berkowitz right from the start.

With much consideration, I have decided upon a much more appropriate penalty for this happy-ass lunatic. It is an ancient Milanese torture protocol called "quaresima," which, when translated to English, means "lent." A member of the

Visconi Dynasty and ruler of Milan, Italy, in the 1300s, Galeazzo II, devised this execution. Notary, chancellor, and judge, Azario, described this torture protocol. Translated below is his description of the execution:

"The intention of the lord is that from the start, the punishment of traitors begins little by little. The first day, five whippings (cinque tratti di curlo) (probably of rope); second day, he rests; The third day another set of five whippings. The fourth day he rests. The fifth day again five whippings. The sixth day, he rests. The seventh day another set of five whippings. The eighth day he rests. The ninth day they shall make him drink water, vinegar and ash. The tenth day he rests. The eleventh day again water, vinegar and ash. The twelfth day he rests. The thirteenth day two strips of skin are taken from the shoulders, and are left to be dripped upon (perhaps by boiling water or oil). The fourteenth day he rests. The fifteenth day the skin from the soles of each foot is removed, then he is made to walk on chickpeas. The sixteenth day he rests. The seventeenth walking on chickpeas. The eighteenth day, he rests. The nineteenth he is placed on the rack. The twentieth he rests. The twenty-first he is placed on the rack. The twenty-second he rests. The twenty-third day they will take an eye out of his head. The twenty-fourth he rests. The twenty-fifth they shall cut his nose off. The twenty-sixth day he rests. The twenty-seventh they shall cut a hand off. The twenty-eighth he rests. The twenty-ninth they shall take the other hand. The thirtieth day he rests. The thirty-first they shall take a foot. The thirty-second he rests. The thirty-third day they shall take the other foot. The thirty-fourth he rests. The thirty-fifth day they shall cut off a testicle. The thirty-sixth day he rests. The thirty-seventh day they shall cut off the other testicle. The thirty-eighth, he rests. The thirty-ninth day they cut off his penis. The fortieth day, he rests. The forty-first he will be attached under a cart, and afterwards placed on the wheel."

Chapter 10

Luis Alfredo Garavito "The Beast"

*So I was born, I do not know why. I felt
pleasure, even though when I had killed
the guilt came over me. —Luis Garavito*

He is pretty much the Colombian version of John Wayne Gacy. They share similar upbringings, perversions, and committed very similar crimes. Luis Alfredo Garavito, or the "Beast," is a brutally cruel, child raping serial killer. Back in 1999, he confessed to the torture, rape, and murder of an astounding 147 boys ranging from 8 to 16 years old over a span of 8 years. However, according to the maps he drew of his various burial sites while in prison, his kill-count may easily exceed 300. These numbers are absolutely staggering. It's unbelievable to think that one man could have single-handedly killed that many people. Regardless, although known as the world's worst serial killer in modern times by some degree, he is completely unheard of by most people.

Not much is known about him, but Garavito was born in 1957, in Genova, Quindío, and was the oldest of seven brothers.

He claims to have been abused by his father, both physically and emotionally, and even claims to have been repeatedly raped by his neighbors. This is yet another case that we could look at and wonder whether if they had grown up differently they would still have committed these crimes.

Luis left home at the age of 16 and never returned. He went on to work various menial jobs to get by, never becoming successful in anything other than becoming an excessive alcoholic. He claimed that he was driven to murder while he was drunk, alleging that he was controlled by a "superior being." Of course, he would certainly not take responsibility for his own actions. Especially when he could just blame it on booze and his imaginary friend. I am guessing Luis was not very bright; this hardly sounds like a reasonable defense.

Around the time of his crimes, Colombia was in turmoil with violence and poverty, and many families were displaced, leaving countless children forsaken to fend for themselves on the streets. Therefore, it is easy to understand how Luis was able to get away with committing so many murders. Targets were not hard for Luis to come by.

Further, his tactic was neither clever nor complex. He often preyed on these poor kids and guttersnipes by gaining their trust after offering them drugs, money, or food. This way, he was easily able to convince these children to go on long walks with him, often making them carry heavy items as they walked. Once the victim grew tired, he attacked; he raped, tortured, then stabbed them to death with a knife or screwdriver, many times slicing their throats and decapitating them.

Many of the bodies that were found had signs of horrible prolonged torture and mutilation. Let me remind you, the oldest of his victims that we know of was 16, the youngest, 8. This man is the epitome of evil, and he deserves nothing less than the nastiest, foulest torture and death conceivable. Tit for tat, as they say.

The Beast's Capture

In 1997, after police came across one of Luis' mass graves containing the mutilated and decapitated bodies of 25 young boys, they formed a nationwide task force. However, they concluded that they were dealing with a satanic cult.

Luis was eventually nabbed in 1999 and charged with over 130 murders while imprisoned for the rape of a 12-year-old boy. Initially, he assumed the identity of a politician in a neighboring city, but after further investigation, the police were able to identify Luis. Once they knew who he was, they found that Garavito had already been on the list of suspects for the bodies found in the mass graves.

Luis confessed immediately during the first interrogation, asking God and mankind for forgiveness. Although he was eventually found guilty, Colombian law limits prison sentencing to a maximum of 40 years for a single person. Nevertheless, due to his cooperation with the police, helping them locate many of the bodies, his sentence was reduced to 22 years. Unbelievably, Garavito was almost released early for good behavior! What's more, when he was interviewed back in 2006, he said that he planned to start a political campaign to help abused children.

When the time came close to his discharge, there was public outcry. Many people thought that Luis deserved a much harsher sentence, many even suggesting that he deserved death. However, during the time of his capture, Colombian law had never before faced such a circumstance. They were not prepared to deal with a criminal case of this magnitude.

In response to this, considering that Luis was already convicted of 130 murders and there were many more that he was not yet charged with in an ongoing case, it is likely that he will now not be released. Unfortunately, he may also never face the death penalty.

During an interrogation, a detective asked Luis if he felt any remorse for what he had done, and he responded by saying that he once felt bad for a kid. While walking with the boy, the kid told Luis about his abusive background. Since Luis had a similar upbringing, he was able to sympathize with the boy. It was a breakthrough, a real bonding experience. Regardless, when Luis got to his preferred location, he tortured and killed the kid anyways.

I think they should have just released him. They do not mess around in Colombia. A merciless horde would lynch Garavito right in front of the prison as he exited the building. He would likely be surrounded by a huge mob and doused with gasoline, and set on fire after being stoned and beaten in the middle of the street. Left bloody and beaten, Garavito would receive the coveted Colombian necktie. This is when a person's throat is cut and their tongue is pulled through the resultant opening, resembling a tie.

Luis Garavito's Medieval Punishment

There are certainly many things that the human mind can think up to seal the fate of Luis Garavito. Whatever torment you could possibly conceive of, it has likely already been done sometime in human history. Some of the most horrible things you may have ever heard of are not creations of the imagination, but reality. Many of the things that you have so far read in this book are absolutely terrible. It takes a sick mind to make some of this shit up.

Mind you, I agree with the assertion that both vicious medieval executions and the serial slaying of innocent children are tragedies. I would rather have a modern-day execution available for someone like the Beast than to not have it at all. At the writing of this book, he lives out his life eating three meals a day and reading science magazines while delighting in the perverted memories of his deeds. Colombia does not have a death penalty; not even for murderers of Luis' caliber.

Nevertheless, I do have a death penalty, and we will relish in the thought of the Beast being mauled and eaten alive by wild animals. To honor his audacious nickname, I choose damnatio ad bestias, also known as *objicĕre bestiis* (to devour by beasts).

This type of capital punishment was implemented by law in Ancient Rome during the time of the near-completion of the Flavian Amphitheatre (later called the Colosseum) in 80 AD.

The amphitheater was a place of worship. Gladiator games were given in honor of the Gods in the hopes of gaining favor for Rome. Depending on the seat, these games sometimes had an admission fee. However, public games were frequently held by campaigning politicians who wanted to earn votes from the plebeians.

Although it had been used prior, damnatio ad bestias was an entertaining sideshow – among many – held at the famous inaugural games. Prior to the main event, many executions and recreations of Roman mythology were also commonly portrayed. This resulted in the death of countless condemned prisoners, slaves, captured soldiers, and Christians.

Ancient theologian Rabanus Maurus Magnentius describes the various methods by which many martyrs of Christianity were subject to execution under Roman dictation. He writes:

"Some were slain with the sword; some burnt with fire; some scourged with whips; some stabbed with forks of iron; some fastened to the cross or gibbet; some drowned in the sea; some had their skins plucked off; some their tongues cut off; some stoned to death; some killed with cold; some starved with hunger; some their hands cut off, or otherwise dismembered, have been so left naked to the open shame of the world."

When the Flavian Amphitheater was erected, it brought this madness and gore to the center stage of Rome. It could hold upwards of 50 to 60 thousand people, with many crammed into the aisle ways. Roman citizens cheered with every splatter of blood. Jeering at the condemned, they bellowed insults and laughed as the arena captives met their death. In one case, it was said that the crowd heckled out *"Salvum lotum!"* when the Christian martyr Saturus' throat was ripped out by a leopard. The translation of their taunt is "Well washed!" They were likely alluding to how his clothes were bathed in his own blood, and poking fun at Christian baptism.

From primary sources of this time, we have uncovered the

diary of Perpetua, one of the Christian martyrs executed with Saturus and others. Perpetua was an educated 22-year-old new mother whose sole crime was that of being a Christian. In 203 AD, while facing prosecution, her father begged her to denounce Christianity to win her freedom and live to care for her newborn baby boy. Refusing to decry her religion, she was happily condemned by the Romans for it. From her writings, we can see that she was delighted to be a martyr. From the book *The Ante-Nicene Fathers: Latin Christianity,* by Alexander Roberts, her diary is recited and translated by Reverend R. E. Wallis:

> "I grieved over the grey hairs of my father, that he alone of all my family would not rejoice over my passion. And I comforted him, saying, 'On that scaffold whatever God wills shall happen. For know that we are not placed in our own power, but in that of God,' And he departed from me in sorrow. Another day, while we were at dinner, we were suddenly taken away to be heard, and we arrived at the town-hall. At once the rumour spread through the neighbourhood of the public place, and an immense number of people were gathered together. We mount the platform. The rest

were interrogated, and confessed. Then they came to me, and my father immediately appeared with my boy, and withdrew me from the step, and said in a supplicating tone, 'Have pity on your babe.' And Hilarianus the procurator, who had just received the power of life and death in the place of the Minucius Timinianus, who was deceased, said, 'Spare the grey hairs of your father, spare the infancy of your boy, offer sacrifice for the well-being of the emperors.' And I replied, 'I will not do so.' Hilarianus said, 'Are you a Christian?' And I replied, 'I am a Christian.' And as my father stood there, cast me down from the faith, he was ordered by Hilarianus to be thrown down, and was beaten with rods. And my father's misfortune grieved me as if I myself had been beaten, I so grieved for his wretched old age. The procurator then delivers judgement on all of us, and condemns us to the wild beasts, and we went down cheerfully to the dungeon."

On the day of execution, Perpetua gracefully walked into the arena with her friend Felicitas by her side. They were both to be killed by a raging bull. They released the bull and it immediately rushed them. It gored Perpetua and dropped her to the ground. Stunned, Perpetua awoke to find that her dress was opened; her modesty was such that she had to fix it. She arose without knowing that the bull already attacked her. The rest of the martyrs gathered together with her in the center of the arena. They kissed and held each other. The crowd grew impatient and chanted for the gladiators to come dispatch of the resilient criminals. A clumsy gladiator approached Perpetua. Without hesitation, as he approached her, he pierced Perpetua's ribs with his sword. She aggressively grabbed his arm and assisted him by bringing the sword to her neck. Directing the anxious gladiator, she violently slashed her own throat.

Perpetua actually got off quite easy. Bulls were sadistically trained to put on a good show. If everything had gone to plan, the bull would have raped her before goring her to death.

Bestiarri is the term used to describe fighters of exotic animals. In some cases, lesser-known gladiators who wanted to make a name for themselves voluntarily became bestiarii. Although the volunteer bestiarius was equipped with armor and weapons, condemned bestiarii were completely naked, totally incapable of defending themselves.

Many different types of exotic animals were in the bestiarii spectacle, including bears, hippos, elephants, bulls, tigers, jaguars, and leopards. So many of these animals were tracked and captured that some species went extinct. In fact, the only bear species known to have inhabited Africa, the atlas bear, no longer exists. As unrealistic as it is, if only we could split this beast Garavito in half and watch as each of his sides ripped himself to pieces. Hell, that scenario might even coin a new term, *ironicus bestiarius.*

In regard to what may have actually happened to Luis Garavito had he been condemned to this fate, of the many beasts that could be chosen as his executioner, one could only hope it to be the wild boar. The Romans starved and beat these animals, ensuring that they would not disappoint on game day. As silly as it may sound, the boar would be last on my list of animals I would choose to fight in the arena.

Considering their diet, wild boars are particularly vicious when they attack people. Boars mainly eat plants and vegetables, meaning that they are not necessarily a predatory animal. Regardless, they will eat anything if they are hungry enough (or hungry at all) and wild boars are known to attack people in many places of the world. Considering that the boar is not very well equipped to subdue large prey, its strategy is to eat. That is how Garavito dies. Literally eaten alive by a 6ft long, 300 to 400 lb. wild boar; a rambunctious, famished animal twice his weight.

From multiple primary sources, a wild boar was originally released on the Christian martyr Saturus. However, the boar was so uncontrollable that it ended up killing one of the Roman guards instead. They had to dispatch of the boar and find another animal to kill with. That should give you an inclination of how ferocious a starving wild boar can be.

While chained to Luis, the boar goes for his legs, eventually getting his foot in its mouth. That is about it for the so-called "Beast." There is nothing poetic about it. The boar eats him as a man eats a carrot. It rips limbs off while Luis despairingly, but futilely, fights back. The boar does not know how to go for vital areas, nor does it care. It just chomps and rips away...

Chapter 11

Albert Fish "The Gray Man"

*Going to the electric chair will be the
supreme thrill of my life. —Albert Fish*

E asily one of the most deranged and perverted serial killers of modern times, Hamilton Howard "Albert" Fish (AKA "The Gray Man" AKA "The Werewolf of Wysteria" AKA "The Vampire of Brooklyn") was an admitted sadomasochistic pedophile, cannibal, and child killer. He stated many times that he enjoyed the flesh of young people, stating that his favorite part was the buttocks, due to its tenderness. Fish was known to brag about having a victim in every state. Factually, we could only be certain that he killed and ate three children. Until his capture at the age of 64, there is no telling how many children Fish actually victimized, but I would not be surprised if that number is in the triple digits.

Randall and Ellen Fish conceived Albert in 1870, with his father being quite elderly when he was born. Randall was 75, and Ellen was approximately 43 years younger. His father was a *'rootin-tootin'* guy, as he continued to have children well into

234

his late 70s. Ironically, his father was a fertilizer manufacturer around the time of Albert's birth. Thus, in more ways than one, he was a major producer of shit. He eventually died in 1875, when Albert was 5 years old, and his mother could not support him anymore. Just like a steaming pile of excrement, he was dumped at an orphanage. It was there that Fish shifted the blame for his sadistic and perverse personality, expounding that his upbringing primed him to become a psycho.

He and many other children within the orphanage were often subject to sexual abuse. Once stripped naked, they were whipped, spanked, and humiliated right in front of each other. Fish later stated that he began to enjoy the pain from these whippings. His mother eventually freed him in 1880 when she became financially secure. Nonetheless, he was not out of the woods as far as weird shit goes.

In 1882, when Fish was 12, he befriended a boy who introduced him to coprophagia (the eating of feces) and urolagnia (the drinking of urine). During the puberty stage of his life, he began to visit public bath houses to watch boys undress, and throughout the rest of his life he wrote disturbing letters to random women whose names he found in public records and classified ads. In 1890, at the age of 20, he became a prostitute, and often raped young boys and street children. Oddly enough, he got married in 1898, and had six children. Not oddly enough, it was an arranged marriage set up by his mother. However, his sacred vows did not deter him from engaging in bizarre sex acts with young men.

Even a simple visit to a waxworks museum fueled his warped sexual fantasies, as he became absolutely captivated by a bisected penis that was put on exhibit. This led him to have a perverse fascination with castration. Now, this tidbit of information may seem like it's inserted here only for shock value, but rest assured, it will become appallingly relevant as you read on. Heed my warning.

In 1903, Fish was arrested for the first time after committing, of all things, grand larceny. He ended up doing a little time in Sing Sing prison. Upon his release, he was in and out of jail and mental institutions for various reasons, including the writing of those disturbing letters and for petty theft.

Around 1910, Albert picked up a 19-year-old mentally challenged man named Thomas Kedden, whom he soon became intimate with. Not long into their relationship, Albert was bored and decided to take Thomas to an old abandoned farmhouse to have a bit of fun. They proceeded to engage in bizarre sex acts, such as eating each other's excrement and performing extreme BDSM scenarios. This lasted a couple weeks until Albert finally decided to tie Thomas to a chair to cut the head of his penis off. With Fish's strange obsession with castration, he wanted to completely dismember him. However, since this was somewhat early in Fish's exploits, the cries of Thomas were too horrifying, and Albert was unable to get the job done. He only sliced halfway into his shaft. Regarding this, Fish later stated, "I shall never forget his scream, or the look he gave me."

Albert had originally planned to kill Thomas and cut him into pieces so he could bring him home, but feared the hot weather would aid the decomposition and rouse suspicions. Instead, he doused Thomas' wounds in peroxide, wrapped him up, and kissed him goodbye as he tossed ten dollars at him, leaving Thomas there in that chair. I compare this to a man who has just finished a sexual liaison with a hooker, tossing a tissue at her while saying, "The money is on the dresser, clean up and get the fuck out."

In 1917, Fish's wife left him for a man that was rooming with them, taking nearly everything he owned, except for the kids. She left her six children to be raised by Albert Fish;

brilliant. It was around this time that he began to indulge in self-harm, and not only shoved 27 pins and needles into his groin and anus, but he also beat himself with a homemade 9" nail-spiked paddle for hours. He even admitted to shoving cotton soaked in lighter fluid into his anus and lighting it on fire. He also said that he stuck a thorny rose stem into his penis and ate it. How someone could talk nonchalantly about doing this to themselves as if it's perfectly normal is absolutely mind-blowing.

Although he did not physically abuse his own kids, he encouraged them and their friends to spank him with his paddle because it sexually stimulated him. Nonetheless, this could be far more psychologically damaging for his children than beating them, in my opinion. Of the vast number of terrible things that you will read about in this book, knowing that he made his own children do that especially gets under my skin. Calling Albert Fish a piece of shit would be an insult to excrement.

Around this time, he gradually became interested in cannibalism, often eating raw meat, and on occasion even feeding it to his kids. He also began to have auditory hallucinations, believing that John the Apostle was speaking directly to him.

A couple of years later, as any normal person who had been thinking God and The Apostle John were talking to them would, Albert became a murderer, often preying on the mentally challenged and blacks. He chose these people because he thought their deaths would receive little attention from the media and they would not be missed. To give you a little bit of insight as to how he spoke about his exploits, Fish described the weapons he used to kill young children with as "implements of Hell." He often carried them around with him in a bag. These implements of Hell consisted of a meat cleaver, a knife, and a hacksaw.

In 1927, Albert went on to abduct, murder, and cannibalize a 4-year-old boy named Billy Gaffney. Fish finally admitted to killing Billy many years later in a letter that he wrote to his lawyer. He graphically described exactly what he did. Here is the unaltered, original text:

> "I brought him to the Riker Ave. dumps. There is a house that stands alone, not far from where I took him....I took the boy there. Stripped him naked and tied his hands and feet and gagged him with a piece of dirty rag I picked out of the dump. Then I burned his clothes. Threw his shoes in the dump. Then I

walked back and took the trolley to 59 St. at 2 A.M. and walked from there home.

Next day about 2 P.M., I took tools, a good heavy cat-of-nine tails. Home made. Short handle. Cut one of my belts in half, slit these halves in six strips about 8 inches long. I whipped his bare behind till the blood ran from his legs. I cut off his ears -- nose --slit his mouth from ear to ear. Gouged out his eyes. He was dead then. I stuck the knife in his belly and held my mouth to his body and drank his blood.

I picked up four old potato sacks and gathered a pile of stones. Then I cut him up. I had a grip with me. I put his nose, ears and a few slices of his belly in the grip. Then I cut him through the middle of his body. Just below the belly button. Then through his legs about 2 inches below his behind. I put this in my grip with a lot of paper. I cut off the head -- feet -- arms-- hands and the legs below the knee. This I put in sacks weighed with stones, tied the ends and threw them into the pools of slimy water you will see all along the road going to North Beach.

I came home with my meat. I had the front of his body I liked best. His monkey and pee wees and a nice little fat behind to roast in the oven and eat. I made a stew out of his ears -- nose -- pieces of his face and belly. I put onions, carrots, turnips, celery, salt and pepper. It was good.

Then I split the cheeks of his behind open, cut off his monkey and pee wees and washed them first. I put strips of bacon on each cheek of his behind and put them in the oven. Then I picked 4 onions and when the meat had roasted about 1/4 hour, I poured about a pint of water over it for gravy and put in the onions. At frequent intervals I basted his behind with a wooden spoon. So the meat would be nice and juicy.

In about 2 hours, it was nice and brown, cooked through. I never ate any roast turkey that tasted half as good as his sweet fat little behind did. I ate every bit of the meat in about four days. His little monkey was a sweet as a nut, but his pee-wees I could not chew. Threw them in the toilet."

After years of torturing, mutilating, and murdering children, an ignorant woman by the name of Estella Wilcox fancied Fish and actually married him. Not surprisingly, they got divorced a week later. One could only guess why, but without a doubt, she discovered something rather unsettling about Albert. Maybe she found a giant razorblade-studded dildo underneath his pillow.

Fish was arrested for harassment after sending another one of his disturbing and perverted letters to a random woman. Subsequently, he was sent to a mental ward for examination. How they could have ever let this man free is beyond my understanding. However, as with most serial killers, Fish was likely very manipulative and effective at concealing his truly monstrous nature.

At 58 years old, he committed one of his most infamous murders of all, the killing and eating of a 10-year-old girl named Grace Budd; this occurred in 1928. It started when Fish responded to a classified ad that said, "Young man, 18, wishes position in country." The ad included the man's name, Edward Budd, and his address. Fish soon appeared at Edwards parents' home for a meeting. Pretending to be a farmer named Frank Howard, Fish said he was willing to hire Edward.

Originally, Albert intended to mutilate Edward in some way or another (probably somewhere near the groin area), leaving him to bleed to death. However, after meeting Edward's younger sister Grace, he instantly changed his mind and decided that he wanted to eat her instead. Sometime after this meeting with the Budds, Albert returned to their house with a cock-and-bull story about a niece's birthday party he was attending and asked if he could take Grace with him; her parents reluctantly agreed. Below is the unaltered letter that Fish sent to Grace's mother, precisely explaining what happened to her thereafter:

> "My dear Mrs Budd
> In 1894 a friend of mine shipped as a deck hand on the steamer Tacoma, Capt John Davis. They sailed from San Francisco to Hong Kong China. On arriving there he and two others went ashore and got drunk. When they returned the boat was gone. At that time there

was a famine in China. Meat of any kind was from \$1–\$3 Dollars a pound. So great was the suffering among the very poor that all children under 12 were sold to the Butchers to be cut up and sold for food in order to keep others from starving. A boy or girl under 14 was not safe in the street. You could go in any shop and ask for steak – chops – or stew meat. Part of the naked body of a boy or girl would be brought out and just what you wanted cut from it. A boy or girls behind which is the sweetest part of the body and sold as veal cutlet brought the highest price. John staid there so long he acquired a taste for human flesh. On his return to N.Y. he stole two boys one 7 one 11. Took them to his home stripped them naked tied them in a closet then burned everything they had on. Several times every day and night he spanked them – tortured them – to make their meat good and tender. First he killed the 11 yr old boy, because he had the fattest ass and of course the most meat on it. Every part of his body was cooked and eaten except Head – bones and guts. He was Roasted in the oven, (all of his ass) boiled, broiled, fried, stewed. The little boy was next, went the same way. At that time I was living at 409 E 100 St, rear – right side. He told me so often how good Human flesh was I made up my mind to taste it. On Sunday June the 3 – 1928 I called on you at 406 W 15 St. Brought you pot cheese – strawberries. We had lunch. Grace sat in my lap and kissed me. I made up my mind to eat her, on the pretense of taking her to a party. You said Yes she could go. I took her to an empty house in Westchester I had already picked out. When we got there, I told her to remain outside. She picked wild flowers. I went upstairs and stripped all my clothes off. I knew if I did not I would get her blood on them. When all was ready I went to the window and called her. Then I hid in a closet until she was in the room. When she saw me all naked she began to cry and tried to run down stairs. I grabbed her and she said she would tell her mama. First I stripped her naked. How she did kick – bite and scratch. I choked her to death then cut her in small pieces so I could take my meat to my rooms, cook and eat it. How sweet and tender her little ass was roasted in the oven. It took me 9 days to eat her entire body."

Fish's Capture

Fish was soon captured even though the letter was made anonymous and with a false name. Police were able to track him by means of investigating the hotel stamp on the paper. Now, considering that he was convicted of writing so many disturbing letters prior, one may assume he would've learned his lesson. From what Fish said, writing for him was a habit that he could not kick. Who knows, had he not taken his perversions to action, he may have become a very successful author of the macabre, like Edgar Allan Poe or H.P. Lovecraft. This would be true if only he had transformed that sinister potency he used to write the Grace Budd letter into works of fiction.

Once apprehended, Fish was subject to extensive psychological examination. The experts stated that although Fish was indeed sane, he was extremely abnormal. Nevertheless, if he was deemed insane, he would not face execution. After witnessing the confessions of Albert Fish, the jurors desperately wanted him to fry.

Fish had an anthology of weird sexual fetishes. These fixations include sadism-masochism, anilingus, cannibalism, coprophagia, urophilia, pedophilia, self-castration, and many others. Although a lot of this stuff was not commonly discussed back then, he was labeled sane. The psychiatrist even said that these odd sexual fetishes were normal, and that most people engage in them. Unlike many inmates who stayed on death row for years, Fish was put to death by the electric chair at Sing Sing prison in January of 1936, after serving only 10 months.

It took two full jolts of electricity to kill him due to the needles that he had shoved up his ass and groin area. That last sentence you read; the oddest factual thing I have ever had to write. Apparently, Fish eagerly walked to the electric chair without needing the aid of an escort, even helping the guards to latch the buckles. It seemed apparent to the reporters that he was looking forward to it.

Once dead, his body was buried at the Sing Sing Prison Cemetery. Fish wrote a lengthy final statement, but his lawyer, James Dempsey, refused to reveal it to anyone due to its extremely disturbing content; "I will never show it to anyone," Dempsey stated, "it was the most filthy string of obscenities that I have ever read." I may be a tad bit morbid, but god damn I would love to read that letter. Damned lawyers... His last words were reportedly, "I don't even know why I'm here," and his last meals were a T-bone steak for lunch and roasted chicken for dinner.

Albert Fish's Medieval Punishment

Now, I have to be careful in my decision-making considering that Fish was a sadomasochist, meaning that he felt sexual arousal while both inflicting pain unto others and enduring his own physical pain. Therefore, I must consider the medieval punishment that would be most fitting for Fish. Not only must he suffer tremendously, inflicting upon him as much agony as humanly possible, but I must also ensure that he does not enjoy a second of it. How unfortunate it is that certain devices similar to the "pear of anguish" must be eliminated from the criteria.

Certainly, the ancient Persian execution method called "scaphism" or "the boats" is most fitting for Albert Fish. This death sentence usually took many days for the person to die, considering the condemned was fed every morning to ensure they lived as long as possible. I must say, this particular torture and execution is one of the most sadistic executions I have heard of as of yet. Below, John Zonoras, a 12th century

Byzantine chronicler, explains it:

> "Two boats are joined together, one on top of
> the other, with holes cut in them in such a way
> that the victim's head, hands, and feet only are
> left outside. Within these boats the man to be
> punished is placed lying on his back, and the
> boats then nailed together with bolts. Next
> they pour a mixture of milk and honey into the
> wretched man's mouth, till he is filled to the
> point of nausea, smearing his face, feet, and
> arms with the same mixture, and so leave him
> exposed to the sun. This is repeated every day,
> the effect being that flies, wasps, and bees,
> attracted by the sweetness, settle on his face
> and all such parts of him as project outside the
> boats, and miserably torment and sting the
> wretched man. Moreover his belly, distended
> as it is with milk and honey, throws off liquid
> excrements, and these, putrefying, breed
> swarms of worms, intestinal and of all sorts.
> Thus the victim lying in the boats, his flesh
> rotting away in his own filth and devoured by
> worms, dies a lingering and horrible death."

According to ancient Greek historian and biographer Plutarch, from his works *Life of Artaxerxes*, a Persian soldier named Mithridates was sentenced to death by scaphism. Bearing an unimaginable 17 days for him to succumb to this terrific execution process, Mithridates suffered one of the foulest deaths in the history of humanity.

The reason for his premature death was certainly trivial, but it appears the circumstances surrounding the event shows that arbitrarily provoked murders were quite common in the ancient Persian Empire at that time. The son of Darius II, Artaxerxes II Mnemon, was crowned king of Persia in 404 BC. Three years into his reign, Artaxerxes' brother, Cyrus the Younger, produced enough soldiers to lead opposition for the throne. Cyrus was certain that the crown was owed to him, and he was willing to kill his own brother for it. These kinds of violent family quarrels were extremely common in this lineage of nobles, as is explained in Plutarch's works. Upon the nearing of Artaxerxes' death, at the age of 94 years old (according to Plutarch), his own sons had a similar feud. This eventually ended in treachery, heartbreak, and murder.

During the battle in 401 BC, Mithridates mistakenly slew Cyrus while he was charging at his countrymen, forcing them on their knees to beg for forgiveness as this noble brother of

Artaxerxes stormed through them. He seemed invincible and imbued with righteousness. Not knowing this was Cyrus, Mithridates shot him in the head with an arrow, knocking him from his horse. In doing so, he unwittingly ended the three-year insurgence once and for all.

Upon hearing of the incident, Artaxerxes ordered Mithridates and the rest of those who were responsible for the death of Cyrus to be inundated with riches. Subsequently, he invited Mithridates to the royal castle to eat and drink with the noble eunuchs. Nevertheless, with the fine wine flowing heavily, Mithridates' boastful tongue led to his demise. In speaking with the eunuchs, Mithridates took full credit for putting an end to the rebellion. He even spoke harshly of the king for not being able to slay Cyrus in battle. Upon hearing this, Artaxerxes did not take kindly to these selfish words. Once these insolent comments escaped his lips, the noble eunuchs knew Mithridates was doomed. For this, not only was Mithridates sentenced to death, but the others responsible for striking Cyrus down that day were ultimately be condemned for similar reasons. Translated to English, Plutarch wrote:

> "After they began to drink, the eunuch that
> was the greatest in power with Parysatis thus
> speaks to him: "A magnificent dress, indeed, O

Mithridates, is this which the King has given you; the chains and bracelets are glorious, and your scymetar of invaluable worth; how happy he has made you, the object of every eye!" To whom he, being a little overcome with the wine, replied, "What are these things, Sparamizes? Sure I am, I showed myself to the King in that day of trial to be one deserving greater and costlier gifts than these." At which Sparamizes smiling, said, "I do not grudge them to you, Mithridates; but since the Grecians tell us that wine and truth go together, let me hear now, my friend, what glorious or mighty matter was it to find some trappings that had slipped off a horse, and to bring them to a king?" And this he spoke, not as ignorant of the truth, but desiring to unbosom him to the company, irritating the vanity of the man, whom drink had now made eager to talk and incapable of controlling himself. So he forbore nothing, but said out, "Talk you what you please of horse-trappings and such trifles; I tell you plainly, that this hand was the death of Cyrus. For I threw not my darts as Artagerses did, in vain and to no purpose, but only just missing his eye, and hitting him right on the temple, and piercing him through. I brought him to the ground; and of that he died." The rest of the company, who saw the end of the hapless fate of Mithridates as if it were already completed, bowed their heads to the ground; and he who entertained them said, "Mithridates, my friend, let us eat and drink now, revering the fortune of our prince, and let us waive discourse which is too weighty for us."

Presently after, Sparamizes told Parysatis what he said, and she told the king, who was greatly enraged at it, as having the lie given him, and being in danger to forfeit the most glorious and most pleasant circumstance of his victory. For it was his desire that every one, whether Greek or barbarian, should believe in mutual assaults and conflicts between him and his brother, he, giving and receiving a blow, was himself indeed wounded, but that the other lost his life. And, therefore, he decreed that Mithridates should be put to death in boats; which execution is after the following manner: Taking two boats framed exactly to fit and answer each other, they lay down in one of them the malefactor that suffers, upon his back; then, covering it with the other, and so setting them together that the head, hands, and feet of him are left outside, and the rest of his body lies shut up within, they offer him food, and if he refuse to eat it, they force him to do it by pricking his eyes; then, after he has eaten, they drench him with a mixture of milk and honey, pouring it not only into his mouth, but all over his face. They then keep his face continually turned towards the sun; and it becomes completely covered up and hidden by the multitude of flies that settle on it. And as within the boats he does what those that eat and drink must needs do, creeping things and vermin spring out of the corruption and rottenness of the excrement, and these entering into the bowels of him, his body is consumed. When the man is manifestly dead, the uppermost boat being taken off, they find his flesh devoured, and swarms of such noisome creatures preying upon and, as it were, growing to his inwards. In this way Mithridates, after suffering for seventeen days, at last expired."

I hardly think that even Albert Fish would have enjoyed any bit of this execution. Although Fish was a sadomasochist, he seemed to only enjoy blunt trauma and sharp, piercing pain. Therefore, I believe this would fly in the face of all that he could relish. If anything in the world could have disturbed Albert Fish, knowing that he would gradually be devoured by worms, maggots, and whatever else that happened to burrow its way into his body as he steeped in a pool of his own urine and diarrhea may have done it. With this type of prolonged death, there would be no thrill to be had.

Chapter 12

H. H. Holmes "Dr. Death"

...the certainty that in a few days I am to be hanged by the neck until I am dead seems but a pastime. —H.H. Holmes

Born in 1861 in New Hampshire, Herman Webster Mudgett, later known as H. H. Holmes, went on to be coined America's first serial killer. Holmes was a particularly bright student even though he was born into a simple farmer's home, with a family lineage of farmers stretching back to the early settlers. He easily graduated High School at the young age of 16. From the little information that we do have, it has been said that his father was a raging alcoholic. I am rather certain this did not help in any way toward the development of Holmes' moral compass. While in grade school, he was teased and ridiculed by less gifted, jealous classmates.

Holmes vividly recounted a day that he was bullied and forced into a nearby doctors' office. He stated that after being cornered, the bullies taunted him with the human skeleton display. They shoved it toward him and made it touch his face.

Holmes stated that after a pithy fright, he was intrigued by the skeleton. He promptly became obsessively fascinated with human anatomy. Holmes even went as far as to say that this was the moment that facilitated an end to all his fears, never to feel that pathetic emotion again. Soon after this experience, Holmes started dissecting any kind of animal he could find. This is very common adolescent serial killer behavior.

Accompanied by his obsession with anatomy, Holmes naturally decided to go into the medical field, barely earning his doctor's degree from the University of Michigan in June of 1884. While in college, Holmes needed to find a way to scrape by and pay his way through school. After spending countless hours studying and dissecting the University's cadavers, Homes devised a genius scheme.

He and a classmate stole corpses and took out false insurance claims on them, forged documents, and made Holmes the beneficiary. This was much more plausible in his day, considering that there were fewer methods of identifying a person's body than there are now. During this time, Holmes formulated another brilliant business venture in which he dug up bodies from cemeteries and sold them to universities as cadavers to be studied and dissected by students. Holmes was on his way to becoming a world-class con artist and scumbag posterchild.

In 1886, Holmes committed his first murder by killing one of his former college classmates, Dr. Robert Leacock. He did this by giving him a lethal dose of a non-prescription drug (at that time), laudanum; a narcotic composed of opium, codeine, and morphine. Although I believe that Holmes did enjoy killing, it appears that he did not kill for pleasure, rather, he killed for profit; for this first murder, he stated that he felt immense remorse. In his own written confession regarding the killing of Dr. Leacock, Holmes wrote:

> "...the risk and excitement attendant upon the collection of the forty-thousand dollars of insurance were very insignificant matters compared with the torturing thought that I had taken human life. This will be understood that before my constant wrong-doing, I had become wholly deaf to the promptings of conscience. For prior to his death, which occurred in 1886, I begged to be believed in stating that I had never sinned so heavily either by thought or deed. Later, like the man-eating tiger of the tropical jungle, whose appetite for blood has once been aroused, I

roamed about the world seeking whom I could destroy."

Thereafter, he began his voyage, conning and killing for profit as he traveled throughout the mid-west until he settled in Chicago within the same year, when Holmes stumbled upon a drugstore owned by Dr. Elizabeth Holton.

Holmes must have loved Chicago. He decided to take up shop and became employed as the drugstore pharmacist. This is where he started going by the alias Dr. Henry H. Holmes. With the profession of killing on the mind, I could completely understand why Chicago would feel like a haven for such a person. It was a vast city with an enormous population of people who were less than familiar with each other.

It was common for someone to up and leave the city, moving away on whims unbeknownst to anyone but themselves. For this reason, when Dr. Elizabeth Holton inexplicably disappeared after the death of her husband, none questioned Holmes when he said that he purchased the drugstore from her, telling customers that she moved "out west." I find this a little hard to believe, but considering that Holmes never confessed to her murder, one could only speculate as to whether or not he killed her. I am going to speculate here and say that he killed her.

While procuring his fortune, Holmes purchased a vacant cottage located across the street from the pharmacy with aspirations of building a grand hotel. Because of its size, taking up the entire block, measuring 162 ft. by 50 ft., locals called the three-story building the "castle."

Although a building of this magnitude would have been difficult for even a much wealthier person, not only did he take out loans that he had no intent of repaying, but he also scammed many contractors, often never paying them for services performed. This magnificent building, arrayed with beautiful stained glass windows, was later described as a "murder castle," operating as Holmes' own human slaughterhouse and cadaver factory.

The first floor was his elegant storefront. With frescos painted on the walls and glistening black and white tiles lining the floors, even the pharmacy was quite impressive. The second and third floor contained Holmes' personal office and over a hundred windowless rooms, stairways leading to nowhere, tilted hallways and doors that could only be opened from one side. The design of the building was intended to cause extreme bewilderment and confusion. The basement had dungeons with blowtorches built into the walls and adjacent lairs equipped with nooses for hanging victims. Killing was a business for Holmes, and he was a workaholic.

Mind you, Holmes was a cunning and meticulous kind of serial killer, and I would be doing a disservice to you by not including the happenings that led up to the construction of this Murder Castle. The kind of con man that Holmes was is astounding, and if you are interested in reading more about his shady business practices then I suggest picking up the book *The Strange Case of Dr. H. H. Holmes.* In it, you can read his autobiography as well as the fully detailed confession letter that he later wrote in prison while awaiting execution.

In his confession, Dr. Holmes proclaims that his second murder occurred after the castle had already been built, but considering his record of accomplishment and the murderous construction of the castle, I can confidently say that this is untrue. Holmes only confessed to 27 murders, all of which he was charged with. He never confessed to any murders that he was not investigated for. Regarding this, Holmes writes:

> "I speak only of the cases that have been thus
> investigated and of no others, I trust it will not

give rise to a supposition that I am still guilty of other murders which I am withholding.

To those inclined to think thus, I will say that the detectives have gone over my entire life, hardly a day or an act has escaped their closest scrutiny, and to judge that I am guilty of more than those cases which they have traced out is to cast discredit upon their work. So marvelous has been the success of these men into whose hands the providing of my guilt was given, that as I look back upon their year's work it seems almost impossible that men gifted with only human intelligence could have been so skillful, and I feel that I can here call attention to what the prosecution at the close of my trial was denied the pleasure of stating, concerning their ability, through no words of mine can fittingly express what the world at large owes to these impartial and untiring representatives, and more especially to Assistant District Attorney Barlow and Detective Frank Geyer and to O. La Forrest Perry, of the Fidelity Mutual Life Association of Philadelphia; for it is principally owing to their unerring judgement, skill and perseverance that in a few days I am forever placed beyond the power of committing other, and, perhaps, if possible, more horrid wrongs."

Pertaining to the death of his second victim, Holmes writes:

"My second victim was Dr. Russell, a tenant in the Chicago building recently renamed "The Castle." During a controversy concerning the non-payment of rent due me, I struck him to the floor with a heavy chair, when he with one cry for help, ending in a groan of anguish, ceased to breathe. This quarrel and death occurred in a small outer office, and as soon as I realized that my blow had been a fatal one and I had recovered somewhat from the horror of having still another victim's blood upon my hands, I was forced to look about for some safe means of concealing the crime."

This is likely a mellowed version of the murder, but his claims of remorse are bullshit. This is after he had already constructed an easily accessible gas chamber in his office to assist his victims to their doom. He politely held their hands as they stepped in before he would slam the vaulted door behind them. After gassing his victim, their body would be dragged through a corridor into a windowless room to be thrown into a large chute leading directly to the basement.

Once there, Holmes utilized two enormous vats, where he placed the cadavers. After dissecting the bodies, one vat was used to remove the flesh with acid and the other to bleach the bones. He sold off their skeletons as display models to universities, one ending up at the prestigious Harvard University, in Cambridge, Massachusetts.

One particularly disturbing murder Holmes was responsible for was the killing of a pregnant woman and her niece. He describes what happened in his own words:

> "Miss Mary Haracamp, of Hamilton, a niece of Mrs. Sarah Cook, came to Chicago and entered my employ as a stenographer. But Mrs. Cook and her niece had access to all the rooms by means of a master key and one evening while I was busily engaged preparing my last victim for shipment, the door suddenly opened and they stood before me. It was a time for quick action, rather than for words of explanation

upon my part, and before they had recovered from the horror of the sight, they were within the fatal vault, so lately tenanted by the dead body, and then, after writing a letter at my dictation to Mr. Cook that they had tired of their life with him and had gone away not expecting to return, their lives were sacrificed instead of giving them liberty in exchange for their promise to an once and forever leave Chicago, which had been promised in return for writing the letter. These were particularly sad deaths, both on account of the victims being exceptionally upright and virtuous women and because Mrs. Sarah Cook, had she lived, would have soon become a mother."

Two days before the World's fair was set to close, the newly elected mayor, Carter Harrison Sr. was assassinated, and the Chicago economy hit a low. Holmes consequently decided to leave the city in search of more methods of swindling and conning his way to riches. He had befriended another con man by the name of Benjamin Pitezel, whom he traveled across the United States with. They successfully committed various acts of insurance fraud and scams.

Holmes' Capture and Execution

Holmes was eventually busted for running a very lucrative racket in which he stole horses from Texas and resold them across the country. This was the first time Holmes had ever been jailed, and considering that he was such a successful scammer, many media outlets clamored for his story. This gave Holmes a bit of notoriety and celebrity as a cunning con man. I believe this was a big motivating factor when he ultimately decided to write his impressively articulate confession.

While in jail, Holmes was celled along with the infamous Wild West gunslinger Marion "The Handsome Bandit" Hedgepeth, who was on his way to serving 25 years for robbing a train. Not surprisingly, while in jail, Holmes came up with yet another scheme to fake his own death and take out a life insurance policy on himself. He was able to sucker Hedgepeth after promising him $500 to refer him to a crooked lawyer who could help execute the plan. Hedgepeth agreed and gave him the information for a lawyer named Jeptha Howe. When Holmes attempted to follow through with the plan, and even though Howe was on board with it, the plan failed, and Holmes decided to abandon it for another one. Just another failed business venture, nothing new for Holmes...

Nevertheless, Holmes' reputation for screwing over his business partners shortly led to his demise. The next plan was to have Pitezel fake his own death and split the $10,000 life insurance money with his wife, Holmes, and the crooked lawyer. Instead, Holmes actually killed Pitezel, collected all of the insurance money, and ran away. He also killed Pitezel's children – two young girls and a boy – fearing that they might eventually expose him. However, in the end, it was these murders that put the noose around his neck. Regarding the murder of Banjamin Pitizel, Holmes confessed:

> "I intended to kill him, and all my subsequent care of him and his, as well as my apparent trust in him by placing in his name large amounts of property, were steps taken to gain his confidence and that of his family so when the time was ripe they would be more readily fall into my hands. It seem almost incredible now that as I look back that I could have expected to have experienced sufficient satisfaction in witnessing their deaths to repay me for even the physical exertion that I had put forth in their behalf during those seven long years, to say nothing of the amount of money I had expended for their welfare, over

and above what I could have expected to receive from his comparatively small life insurance. Yet, so it is, and it furnishes a very striking illustration of the vagaries in which the human mind will, under certain circumstances, indulge; in comparison with which the seeking of buried treasure at the rainbow's end, the delusions of the exponents of perpetual motion. Pitezel left his home for the last time in July, 1894, a happy, light-hearted man, to whom trouble or discouragements of any kind were almost unknown. We then journeyed together to New York and later to Philadelphia, where the fatal house upon Callowhill Street in which he met his death September 2, 1894, was hired. Then came my writing to him the discouraging letters, purporting to be from his wife, causing him to again resort to drink. Then the waiting from day to day until I should be sure of finding him in a drunken stupor at midday. This was an easy matter, as I was acquainted with his habits and so sure was I of finding him thus incapacitated that when the day came upon which it was convenient for me to kill him, even before I went to his house, quietly unlocked the door, stole noiselessly within and to the second story room, where I found him insensibly drunk, as I had expected. But even in this condition the question may be asked had I no fear that he might be only naturally asleep or partly insensible and therefore liable to at any moment come to his senses and defend himself? I answer no, and that even had he done so my great strength would have enabled me to have still overpowered him.

Only one difficulty presented itself. It was necessary for me to kill him in such a manner that no struggle or movement of his body should occur or otherwise his clothing being in any way displaced it would have been impossible to again put them in a normal condition. I overcame this detail by first binding him hand and foot and having done I proceeded to burn him alive by saturating his clothing and his face with benzene, igniting it with a match. So horrible was this torture that in writing of having been tempted to attribute his death to some humane means—not with wish to spare myself, but because I fear that it will not be believed less, by excursion, the authorities have determined for me that his death could only have occurred in this manner, no blows or bruises upon his body and drug administered, save chloroform, which was not placed in his stomach until at least 30 minutes after his death, and to now make a misstatement of the facts would only serve to draw out additional criticism from them. The least I can do is spare my reader a recital of the victim's cries for me, his prayers and finally, his plea for a more speedy termination of sufferings, all of which upon me had no effect. Finally, he was removed from the straps and ropes that had bound him and I extinguished the flames, and a little later, poured into his stomach one and one half ounces chloroform. It has been asked why I did this after I knew he was dead, what possible use could it have served? My answer to this is that I placed it there so that at the time of the post mortem examination, which I knew was to be held, the Coroner's physician would be warranted in the reporting that death was accidental, and due to an explosion of a cleaning fluid, composed of benzene and chloroform, and that the chloroform had at the time of explosion separated from the benzene and passed into his stomach and receipt of such intelligence I believed the insurance company would at once pay full amount of the claim."

The murders of Pitizels' children are particularly disturbing. First, he killed the eight-year-old boy, Howard Pitezel. Holmes described how he did it in this unsettling confession:

"On October 7 I called at the Irvington drug store and purchased the drugs I needed to kill the boy and the following evening I again went to the same store and bought an additional supply, as I feared I had not obtained a sufficient quantity upon my first visit. My next step was to secure the furniture for the house. This was done upon October 8, late in the afternoon, at such an hour that made it impossible for the store owner to deliver them, and as I wished to stay at Irvington that night I hired a conveyance and carted the goods to the house myself, keeping the horse there until the next day. It was also upon the 8th, early in the forenoon, that I went to the repair shop for the long knives I had previously left there to be sharpened. Early in the afternoon of October 10th, I had the boy's trunk and a stove I had brought taken to the depot, and they arrived at the Irvington house at about 6P.M. at which time Mr. Moreman was the last person who saw the boy alive, for almost immediately I called him into the house and insisted that he go to bed at once, first giving him a fatal dose of medicine. As soon as he had ceased to breathe I cut his body into pieces that would pass through the door of the stove and by the combined use of gas and corncobs proceeded to burn it with as little feeling as 'tho it had been some inanimate object."

He killed both of the girls, Alice and Nellie, at the same time, forcing both of them inside a large trunk to stay in for hours before drilling a hole into the top of it and then inserted a hose that released toxic gases:

> "Later than 8:00 P.M. I again returned to the
> house where the children were imprisoned,
> and ended their lives by connecting the gas
> with the trunk, then came the opening of the
> trunk and the viewing of their little blackened
> and distorted faces, then the digging of their
> shallow graves in the basement of the house,
> the ruthless stripping off of their clothing and
> the burial without a particle of covering save
> the cold earth, which I heaped upon them with
> fiendish delight. Consider what an awful act
> this was! These little innocent and helpless
> children, the oldest only being 13 years of age,
> a puny and sickly child, who to look at one
> would believe much younger"

These unforgivable acts soon came to light after Holmes
was ratted out by none other than his old cellmate, gunslinger
Marion Hedgepeth, when Holmes failed to come through with
the $500 he was owed. Marion directed investigators to the
attorney, who gave Holmes up without hesitation.

Originally only charged with insurance fraud, Holmes was

later connected to Pitezel's murder. It was here that Holmes eventually gave his testimony and confessed to killing 27 people. He detailed the confessions that you have been able to sample here. In 1896, the state of Philadelphia put Holmes to death by hanging.

Hanging has been a method of execution since ancient times and is the preferred method of execution of many countries today. Judicially, there are four different methods: suspension, short drop, standard drop, and long drop. Suspension is the most painful. It is the equivalent of kicking a bucket from under your feet. Essentially, the victim slowly dies from intense strangulation. Thinking about it, you might think that the hanging man loses consciousness immediately, similar to a chokehold. However, this is not the case.

Before his execution, he gave advice to the inexperienced executioner. He told him to take his time, and to make sure he did not bungle it. Wise words from an experienced hangman? It was reported that it took a total of 15 minutes for Holmes to die, but other sources – such as the Philadelphia Weekly – claimed that he died immediately and without pain. The Prison buried Holmes ten feet into the ground and enclosed him in cement, per his request. Perhaps he was worried about grave robbers. Holmes' last meal consisted of boiled eggs with toast and coffee.

Dr. H. H. Holmes' Medieval Punishment

Holmes once claimed that he was fearless. Well, if he were born a couple of centuries prior, he would have had a lot to be afraid of while awaiting execution. Although execution by hanging has existed for thousands of years – and is practiced today as a common form of capital punishment – this would definitely not be the fortunate circumstance for Dr. Holmes.

In his confession, Holmes described seeing himself as disfigured while looking in the mirror. He mentioned that he began to see himself with an elongated face and distortedly evil appearances. He began to think that he was turning into the Devil himself, stating in his own words:

> "I am convinced that since my imprisonment I have changed woefully and gruesomely from what I was formerly in feature and figure. My features are assuming a pronounced satanical cast. I have become afflicted with that dread disease, rare but terrible, with which physicians are acquainted, but over which they have no control whatsoever. That disease

is a malformation or distortion of the osseous parts... My head and face are gradually assuming an elongated shape. I believe fully that I am growing to resemble the devil-that the similitude is almost completed."

With such revelation, a fitting punishment for this devil is that which the Iroquois did to the Huron prisoners of war during their great conflict in Canada. What they did was throw boiling water on the prisoners and roast them atop charred coals for up to six days. Next, they take the victim and start to cut them in extremely sensitive areas of their body, eventually chipping through the skull and removing the brain. One disturbingly detailed account that occurred in 1649 is vividly described in *History of the Early Missions in Early Canada* (1893), written by William Richard Harris. Explaining exactly what happened to a captured French Jesuit missionary by the name of Jean De Brébeuf, taken from the diary of an escaped missionary, Christophe Regnaut, it reads:

"FATHER Jean de Brébeuf and Father Gabriel L`Alemant had set out from our cabin, to go to a small Village, called St. Ignance, distant from our cabin about a short quarter of a league, to instruct the Savages and the new Christians of that Village. It was on the sixteenth Day of March, in the morning, that we perceived a great fire at the place to which these two good Fathers had gone. This fire made us very uneasy; we did not know whether it were enemies, or if the fire had caught in some of the huts of the village. The Reverend Father Paul Ragueneau, our superior, immediately Resolved to send someone to learn what might be the cause. But no sooner had we formed the design of going there to see, than we perceived several savages on the road, coming straight toward us. We all thought it was the Iroquois who were coming to attack us; but, having considered them more closely, we perceived that they were Hurons who were fleeing from the fight, and who had escaped from the combat. [T]hese poor savages caused great pity in us. They were all covered with wounds. One had his head fractured; another his arm broken; another had an arrow in his eye; another had his hand cut off by a blow from a hatchet. In fine, the day was passed in receiving into the cabins all these poor wounded people, and in looking with compassion toward the fire, and the place where were those two good Fathers. We saw the fire and the barbarians, but we could not see anything of the two Fathers.

This is what these savages told us of the taking of the Village of St. Ignace, and about Fathers Jean de Brébeuf and Gabriel L'Allemant:

"The Iroquois came, to the number of twelve hundred men; took our village, and seized Father Brébeuf and his companions; and set fire to all the huts. They proceeded to vent their rage on those two Fathers; for they took them both and stripped them entirely naked, and fastened each to a post. They tied both of their hands together. They tore the nails from their fingers. They beat them with a shower of blows from cudgels, on the shoulders, the loins, the belly, the legs, and the face,—there being no part of their body which did not endure this torment." The savages told us further, that, although Father de Brebeuf was overwhelmed under the weight of these blows, he did not cease continually to speak of God, and to encourage all the new Christians who were captives like himself to suffer well, that they might die well, in order to go in company with him to Paradise. While the good Father was thus encouraging these good people, a wretched Iron renegade,—who had remained a captive with the Iroquois, and whom Father de Brébeuf had formerly instructed and baptized,—hearing him speak Paradise and Holy Baptism, was irritated, and said to him, "Echon," that is Father de Brébeuf's name in Huron, "thou sayest that Baptism and the sufferings of this life lead straight to Paradise; though wilt go soon, for I am going to baptize thee, and to make thee suffer well, in order to go the sooner to thy Paradise." The barbarian, having said that, took a kettle full of boiling water, which he poured over his body three different times, in derision of Holy baptism. And, each time that he baptized him in this manner, the barbarian said to him, with bitter sarcasm, "Go to Heaven, for thou art well baptized." After that, they made him suffer several other torments. The 1st was to make hatchets red-hot, and to apply them to the loins and under the armpits. They made a collar of these red-hot hatchets, and put it on the neck of this good Father. This is the fashion in which I have seen the collar made for the prisoners: They make six hatchets red-hot, take a large with of green wood, pass the 6 hatchets over the large end of the with, take two ends together, and then put it over the neck of the sufferer. I have seen no torment which more moved me to compassion than that. For you see a man, bound naked to a post, who, having this collar on his neck, cannot tell what posture to take. For, if he lean forward, those above his shoulders weigh the more on him; if he lean back, those n his stomach make him suffer the same torment; if he keep erect, without leaning to one side or the other, the burning hatchets, applied equally on both sides, give him a double torture.

After that they put him on a belt of bark, full of pitch and resin, and set fire to it, which roasted his whole body. During all these torments, Father de Brébeuf endured like a rock, insensible to fire and flames, which astonished all the bloodthirsty wretches who tormented him. His zeal was so great that he preached continually to these infidels, to try to convert them. His executioners were enraged against him for constantly speaking to them of God and of their conversion. To prevent him from speaking more, they cut off his tongue and both his upper and lower lips. After that, they set themselves to strip the flesh from his legs, thighs, and arms, to the very bone; and them put it to roast before his eyes, in order to eat it.

While they tormented him in this manner, those wretches derided him, saying "Thou seest plainly that we treat thee as a friend, since we shall be the cause of thy Eternal happiness; thank us, then, for these good offices which we render thee,—for, the more thou shalt suffer, the more will thy God reward thee."

Those butchers, seeing that the good Father began to grow weak, made him sit down on the ground; and one of them, taking a knife, cut off the skin covering his skull. Another one of those barbarians, seeing that the good Father would soon die, made am opening in the upper part of his chest, and tore out his heart, which he roasted and ate. Others came to drink his blood, still warm, which they drank with both hands,—saying that Father Brébeuf had been very courageous to endure so much pain as they had given him, and that, by drinking his blood, they would become courageous like him."

The description of Jean de Brébeuf's execution is quite unsettling, considering that he was an innocent man simply attempting to bring his gospel to the Huron people. Christophe Regnaut later described what he found when he came back to collect Brébeuf's remains:

"Father de Brébeuf had his legs, thighs and arms stripped of flesh to the very bone. I saw and touched a large number of great blisters which he had on several places on his body, from the boiling water which these barbarians had poured over him in mockery of holy baptism. I saw and touched the wound from a belt of bark, full of pitch and resin, which roasted his whole body. I saw and touched the marks of burns from the collar of axes placed on his shoulders and stomach. I saw and touched his two lips, which they cut off because he constantly spoke of God whilst they made him suffer. I saw and touched all parts of his body, which had received more than two hundred blows from a stick. I saw and touched the top of his scalped head; I saw and touched the opening which these barbarians had made to tear out his heart."

This seems to be a fantastic end to the life of such a despicable human being as Dr. H. H. Holmes. For his complete lack of compassion, and his greedy motives for treating people like less than cattle, I think we can do one better. Rather than simply chipping through his skull or ripping out his heart, there needs to be a symbolic method to end this wretch's life.

For this, I choose the lead sprinkler. This harmless-sounding device is quite the opposite. It is a handled metal rod with a spherical ladle at the end of it. The ladle is filled with many different types of boiling liquids and molten metals. In cases such as some recorded from ancient Mongolia, the ladle was filled with molten silver and poured into the sufferer's eyes. The liquid eventually killed the victim by way of dissolving through the flesh and melting the brain. This treatment is opulently fitting for the mercilessly greedy Dr. H. H. Holmes.

287

CONCLUSIONS

Life itself is neither good nor evil, but a
place for good and evil. —Marcus
Aurelius

Good and bad, pious and evil, benevolent and malevolent. Could these characteristics exist within every person? Is being evil a thought, an action, or a conviction? Why is benevolence so fragile? So easily ripped away, one does not have to act out their transgressions to lose it. Merely disclosing their dark identity is enough to expose maliciousness to the hungry virtuous jackal. Throughout history, the subjectivity of morality has been weaponized, hijacked to wage war against the malevolent boogeyman. Whether through religion, government, or social classes, we have demonized the darkness that lurks within man. Fighting the "demons" that live within us, we are forced to bury the shadows that make our identities whole.

Understanding the pattern in the backgrounds of these serial killers, it's easy to empathize with them. If someone experienced a brain injury that made them predisposed to murder, then we have our excuse. That does not explain why they did it. With every action, big or small, we have a choice.

Gacy's father did not make Gacy Jr. kill, the same way that Pichushkin's brain injury did not make him kill. These were conscious decisions made by minds that were in touch with their own morbid nature. They were made monsters by acting out their inner monstrosity.

All truly moral people are monsters underneath. They are not moral because they are good; they are good because they are moral. Many people grew up in much worse conditions than all of the subjects in this book. However, the decision to live in a non-destructive way is a choice that they have made. As does anyone else who explores the darkness of their nature. Knowing that they are capable of truly horrific things, people who understand the wickedness of humanity explore evil in a very personal way. Rather than glorifying fictional murderers, truly morbid people spend their time humoring the tragic realities of the world. Renowned psychiatrist Carl Gustav Jung examined this concept at length, saying:

> "If you imagine someone who is brave enough
> to withdraw all his projections, then you get an
> individual who is conscious of a pretty thick
> shadow. Such a man has saddled himself with
> new problems and conflicts. He has become a

serious problem to himself, as he is now unable to say that they do this or that, they are wrong, and they must be fought against. He lives in the "House of the Gathering." Such a man knows that whatever is wrong in the world is in himself, and if he only learns to deal with his own shadow he has done something real for the world. He has succeeded in shouldering at least an infinitesimal part of the gigantic, unsolved social problems of our day."

We can empathize with many of these serial killers because we are able to place ourselves in their story. We remember the time we were bullied and beaten and the time that we bullied and beat another. We remember when we killed an insect or animal out of sheer curiosity. Knowing that a darkness lives within us, and being able to control it, is the very essence of what it means to be a good, moral person. Otherwise, without the exploration of such evil within oneself, being incapable of any maliciousness, we are nothing more than a domesticated house pet. Being incapable of anything but moral behavior is not benevolence. It is plain existence, without the will to choose between good and evil. On this basis, choice matters, because only then are consequences appropriate. If we are to believe some serial killers when they say that they had no choice but to murder, then consequences may be put into question. They propose that they did not have the will to decide either way, so they are not to blame for their actions. It's a scheme used by manipulators attempting to influence the perceptions of their critics.

Knowing that their choice to kill was deliberate and avoidable, the penalties rendered in this book should be applicable, if not debatable. The medieval tortures and executions portrayed in this book are not recommendations for the treatment of serial killers. They are merely explorations of the darkness that exists within all humanity.

BIBLIOGRAPHY

The Psychopath: Spock, Star Trek, season 3, episode 7 ("Day of the Dove" 1968).

The Psychopath: Dwight Schrute, *"The Office"*, season 2, episode 5, *"Halloween"*, (2005)

The Psychopath: Kocsis, *"Serial Murder and the Psychology of Violent Crimes"*), pg. 4, (2008)

The Psychopath: Kocsis, *"Serial Murder and the Psychology of Violent Crimes"*), pg. 5, (2008)

The Psychopath: Millon, *"Psychopathy: Antisocial, Criminal and Violent Behaviors"*, pg. 155, (1998)

The Psychopath: Staff (September 4, 1994). *"Shootings Seal Post Office Rep"*. Chicago Sun Times – via HighBeam Research (subscription required). (Retrieved Jan. 14, 2017).

Causality: Serial Murder: Multi-Disciplinary Perspectives for Investigators, BEHAVIORAL ANALYSIS UNIT, NATIONAL CENTER FOR THE ANALYSIS OF VIOLENT CRIME, Critical Incident Response Group, Federal Bureau of Investigation, (Retrieved August 26, 2016) from https://www.fbi.gov/stats-services/publications/serial-murder#three

Classification: Aamodt, M. G. (2015, November 23). Serial killer statistics. (Retrieved Nov. 23, 2015) from http://maamodt.asp.radford.edu/serial killer information center/project description.htm

Brief History of Torture: Jiu-Hwa L. Upshur, *"World History"*, Cengage Advantage Books (fifth Edition), (2012), pg 23
Brief History of Torture: Livy, *"The History of Rome"*, 35.18

Brief History of Torture: Nathaniel Hooke, *"The Roman History: From the Building of Rome to the Ruin of the Commonwealth"*, (1830), pg 499

Brief History of Torture: Suetonius, *"The Lives of Twelve Caesars"*, Life of Tiberius, 60-62

Brief History of Torture: Charles George Habermann, *"The Catholic Encyclopedia: An International Work of Reference on the Constitution, Doctrine, Discipline, and History of the Catholic Church, Volume 8"*, Encyclopedia Press, (1913), pg 32

Brief History of Torture: Phillippus van Limborch, *"The History of the Inquisition; with a Particular Description of Its Secret Prisons, Modes of Torture, Etc.; Abridged from the Work of P.L.; Introduced by an Historical Survey of the Christian Church, Etc"*, (1816)

Brief History of Torture: Richard Krafft-Ebing, *"Psychopathia Sexualis"*, F.A. Davis Company, (1894), pg. 86-87

John Wayne Gacy: Tom Philbin, *"Killer Book of Serial Killers"*, Sourcebooks, (2009)
Gacy, Impalement: Vlad the Impaler (Dracula) Vlad Tepes, http://www.medievality.com/vlad-the-impaler.html

John Wayne Gacy, Impalement Crowley, *1453: The Holy War for Constantinople and the Clash of Islam and the West*, pp. 153-154).

Alexander Pichushkin, Spanish Inquisition: William Harris Rule, *"History of The Inquisition from Its Establishment in the Twelfth Century to Its Extinction in the Nineteenth"*, University of Michigan Library, (1874)

Ted Bundy: Tom Philbin, *"Killer Book of Serial Killers"*, Sourcebooks, (2009)

Ted Bundy: Eneas Sweetland Dallas, *"Once a Week"*, Bradbury and Evans, January, 1 1866, *"Old Times in Jamaica"*, (May 26, 1866)

Ted Bundy: Mark P. Donnely Daniel Diehl, "The Big Book of Pain", The History Press, (2013), pg. 204-205

Ted Bundy: Daniel P. Mannix, *"The History of Torture"*, Dell Publishing, (1964), pg. 114-115

Ted Bundy: S. C. Turnbo, *"Flayed Alive by Indians"*, Brother Jonathan, (September 1859)

Ted Bundy: Rev A. C. Zenos, D.D, *"The Ecclesiastical History of Socrates Scholasticus.* Revised, with Notes", pg. 293, (1886)

Luis Alfredo Garavito: "*World: Americas Colombian Child Killer Confesses*", (October 30 1999), BBC News (BBC Online Network), http://news.bbc.co.uk/2/hi/americas/493887.stm

Luis Alfredo Garavito: Juan Ignacio Blanco, http://murderpedia.org/male.G/g/garavito.htm

Luis Alfredo Garavito, Damnatio ad Bestias: http://www.softschools.com/facts/animals/wild_boar_facts/314/ (2005-2015 Softchools.com)

Luis Alfredo Garavito, Damnatio ad Bestias: Alexander Roberts, The Ante-Nicene Fathers: Latin Christianity: its founder, Tertullian. I. Apologetic; II. Anti-Marcion; III. Ethical, C. Scribner's Sons, (1903)

Luis Alfredo Garavito, Damnatio ad Bestias*: Clark, D.W., Wasgatt, Davis, *Death-bed Scenes: Or, Dying with and Without Religion,* (1851)

Edmund Kemper: Scott Bonn, "*Why We Love Serial Killers*", Skyhorse Publishing, (2014)

Edmund Kemper: Elliot Leyton, "*Hunting Humans*", Blake Publishing, (2001)

Edmund Kemper, Diodorus Siculus, "*Delphi Complete Works of Diodorus Siculus*", "*Bibliotheca Historica*", *Vol IV,* Delphi Classics; 1 edition, (2014)

Dennis Rader: Wenzl, Potter, Kelly, "*Bind, Torture, Kill: The Inside Story of the Serial Killer Next Door*", Harper Collins, (2006)

Dennis Rader: Trevor Marriott, "*The Evil Within - A Top Murder Squad Detective Reveals The Chilling True Stories of The World's Most Notorious Killers*", John Blake Publishing, (2013)

Dennis Rader: Janet McClellan, "*Erotophonophilia: Investigating Lust Murder*", Cambria Press, (2010)

Dennis Rader, William Wallace: Henry Smith Williams, "*Scotland, Ireland, England Since 1792*", (1908)

Dennis Rader, William Wallace: John Reuben Davies, "The Execution of William Wallace: Saint Bartholomew's Eve, Monday 23 August 1305", Feature of the Month (August 2013), _The Breaking of Britain: Cross-

Border Society and Scottish Independence 1216 1314_, on line at http://www.breakingofbritain.ac.uk/blogs/feature-of-the-month/august-2013/ (accessed 30 December 2015)

John Reuben Davies, *"The Execution of William Wallace: the Earliest Account"*, Feature of the Month (May 2011), _The Breaking of Britain: Cross-Border Society and Scottish Independence 1216–1314_, on line at http://www.breakingofbritain.ac.uk/blogs/feature-of-the-month/may-2011-the-execution-of-william-wallace/ (accessed 30 December 2015)

Dennis Rader: William Wallace: Sir Frederick Pollock, Frederic William Maitland, *"The History of English Law Before the Time of Edward I"*, (Volume II), (1898)

David Berkowitz: Scott Bonn, *"Why We Love Serial Killers"*, Skyhorse Publishing, (2014)

David Berkowitz, Quaresima: Larissa Tracy, *"Torture and Brutality in Medieval Literature: Negotiations of National Identity"*, D S Brewer, (2012)

Albert Fish, Mithridates: Plutarch, *"Delphi Complete Works of Plutarch"*, *"Life of Artaxerxes II"*, Delphi Classics; 1 edition (2013)

H. H. Holmes: Herman Mudgett, *"The Strange Case of Dr. H. H. Holmes"*, Waterfront Productions, (2005), (Original Autobiography 1895)

H. H. Holmes, Jean de Brébeuf: Aaron M. Shatzman, *"The Old World, the New World, and the Creation of the Modern World, 1400-1650: An Interpretive History"*, Anthem Press, pg. 130, (2013)

H. H. Holmes, Jean de Brébeuf: William Richard Harris, *"History of the Early Missions in Western Canada"*, Hunter Rose, (1893)

Printed in Great Britain
by Amazon

41207638R00173